THE LIFE OF A
Spoiled BRAT

MARY JEAN ROSE

ISBN 978-1-0980-7105-9 (paperback)
ISBN 978-1-0980-7106-6 (digital)

Copyright © 2020 by Mary Jean Rose

All rights reserved. No part of this publication may be reproduced, distributed, or transmitted in any form or by any means, including photocopying, recording, or other electronic or mechanical methods without the prior written permission of the publisher. For permission requests, solicit the publisher via the address below.

Christian Faith Publishing, Inc.
832 Park Avenue
Meadville, PA 16335
www.christianfaithpublishing.com

Printed in the United States of America

PART 1

A Spoiled Brat Grows Up

It was grace, mercy, and divine guidance that got me to this age in spite of myself. At eighty-one, I know less than I did when I was sixteen. Then I knew I could solve all the world's problems. *If they would only listen to me.* Life seemed so simple then.

Thinking back over my life, the world I was born into had no electricity, telephones, indoor plumbing, running water, automobiles, computers, or television. Our bathroom was a two-seater shed out in back. Transportation was horse and wagon. Lights were candles or kerosene lanterns with wicks that required trimming and needed to be lit. We did have farmer matches. Refrigeration was an underground dugout in the yard. We called it a root cellar. Heat was the wood cookstove. That meant cutting down trees, sawing them into pieces that fit into the stove, and hauling them to a pile near the house. Someone had to bring them inside to the wood box as needed. Dad always said wood headed him three times. Once when he cut it, once when he hauled it in, and then again, when it burned in the stove.

Mother baked wonderful bread and pies in the oven of that woodstove. She was a great cook and baker. Water came from a hand pump, the one you had to pump the handle up and down. Sometimes it required pouring water into to it to prime it. Mother did the laundry on a washboard at the sink and had to heat the water in a large tub on the cookstove.

Some people in town had electricity and automobiles. Some had indoor plumbing and hanging on the wall crank telephones. I must have been about five when we borrowed my uncle's car so we didn't have to take the horses to town. Soon Dad collected parts and built a tractor of his own. He called it the doodle bug.

My very first memory is standing on a wooden kitchen chair at the sink, excited to help Mother with the dishes. Don't remember, but I must have been three or four. Mother was wearing a faded print house dress made from feed sacks. The cream-colored apron she wore was streaked with dust and dirt. At least it covered most of her dress. I was wearing a bright flower-printed play dress. My strawberry blond hair hung slightly wavy and stringy. Mother's was the same color. Hers was short, curlier, and messed up from a hard day's work. My clear blue-green eyes matched hers, except hers were tired from a hard day of trying to make that little house into something nice for us. She was average build but muscular for a woman from working with Dad on the farm. She had fired the wood cookstove with plenty of wood to make a hot fire for heating the water in the tea kettle after she pumped it from the hand pump at the sink. When it was hot, she poured it into two basins in the sink and mixed it with cold water to make it the right temperature, one to wash and one to rinse. After she rinsed the clean dishes in the rinse water, she put them on the drainboard to dry. From there, I attempted to dry them with a towel made from feed sacks.

Then I heard my dad say, "There's a wasp nest in the wall."

We had just moved into the small one-room house that smelled musty and still needed finishing. The house was a simple board house with unfinished stud walls inside. The roof of rolled black tar paper roofing protected us from the rain. The outside was black tar paper. I guess some would call it a tar paper shack. To me it was home, but even though the inside was not finished, it had a wood cookstove, a cabinet big enough to hold the large sink with a drainboard, and alongside, a hand pump. I also remember my small bed in a corner and a hide-a-bed couch where my parents slept, plus a round wooden table with wooden spindle-back chairs. I don't think there was room for much more. Outside the door was an attached shed where the wood for the stove was kept.

That evening, Dad was in his farmer overalls nailing boards to the inside of the walls. When he mentioned the wasp nest, I jumped off the chair, towel in my hand, and ran to my dad saying, "What's a wasp nest?"

Dad pointed to it and responded, "That's it. Stay back, there could be a wasp inside."

I stepped closer. Just then a wasp flew out directly at me. I swung the dish towel at it.

Dad said, "Don't swing at it. You could make it mad."

I was determined to get rid of it by swinging the towel in my hand around, trying to chase it away. It landed on the towel. I thought I could shake it off by swinging the towel around. It got off all right. It landed on my arm and stung me. I screamed. Crying because I was hurt and humiliated, I ran to my mother. I now knew to stay away from wasp nests, but it hadn't occurred to me that I should listen to my father.

We had an outhouse and a bucket in the house in case we didn't want to go out in the dark or the rain. A couple hundred feet behind the house was a shed for the cows and chickens.

I was a happy kid. My dad was my buddy. I thought he looked like what I thought a prince would look like. His black short hair, his dark blue-gray eyes. He was six feet tall. He wore his farmer overalls everywhere and stood tall and proud. I followed him whenever I could. He called me his helper. I pretty much got everything I wanted.

When Dad was planting something, I would follow along. He soon had me carrying things for him. I was so important. I didn't have much for toys, but life was so full of fun and discovering things that I was seldom bored.

In the evening, the cows needed to be brought in from the back pasture. Our dog, Shep, a black and white English shepherd, would go with me and Dad. Shep did most of the work bringing the cows home if we just encouraged him a little. I still can't get over how he would go behind the cows and walk back and forth barking only occasionally. The cows would simply walk slow and easy toward home. Shep was my best friend and had the run of the farm. He slept in the woodshed at night and ran free during the day. He and I did most everything together when I wasn't helping my dad.

Once when we were out bringing in the cows, Dad pointed out a big buck deer with a big rack of antlers. It was just across the field. Shep and I wanted to run and catch the deer, but when the deer saw us, he ran away. Even so, that picture will be forever etched in my mind. He still is one of the most beautiful creatures I have ever seen.

Getting the cows in provided much entertainment, like the day Dad, myself, and Shep crossed the little board bridge made from logs with planks over them, just wide enough for the tractor to cross over the creek on our farm.

Dad said, "Look down there." In the water of the shallow creek was a small, pretty rainbow trout just lazing down the creek. I laid on my tummy on the bridge and watched the fish until Dad said we needed to get going.

Sometimes I picked wildflowers along the way. In season, one could pick wild blackberries.

One day, Dad said, "You and Shep can go get the cows today. You know the way, and Shep will do the work. Just stay on the foot path through the woods."

So Shep and I went out to get the cows. Of course, I had to stop at the bridge and look for fish. Shep was not happy with me and tried to get me going by barking and nudging me. As we walked down the path through the woods, a short distance later, I head a funny noise, a sort of rattle. I wanted to go see what it was. In my head, I heard my dad say, *Stay on the path.* I took a step off the path and saw something all coiled up with a head and tail sticking up, the tail rattling, the head hissing. Shep grabbed on to the hem of my dress and pulled on me. He wouldn't let me go closer. I was not happy with him because I wanted to get a better look.

I said, "I just want to see it better. I will be right by the path."

He wouldn't let go and kept tugging on me. I gave up. We went on to get the cows. Shep brought them home while I meandered along behind.

When I told Mom and Dad about what happened, they said, "It must have been a rattlesnake. Never go near them. They could bite you, and you could die."

After that, they didn't let me go alone, or even with Shep, to get the cows for some time. Thinking back, I must have had a guardian angel.

One day, I decided it was not fair that I couldn't go by myself to bring in the cows. It was midday, but I didn't pay attention to time. I thought, *I will go get the cows in and show Mom and Dad that I can. Shep will go with me.* Shep was my constant companion. That day, the cows seemed confused and went a different way. I remember walking down the creek bed. It was dry, probably because it was late summer. Maybe the cows were looking for water. At one point, the cows went out of the creek and into the woods. Shep followed. I became confused and didn't know what to do. I sat down and cried. Maybe I fell asleep. Next thing I knew, Dad was there. He seemed really happy to see me, but as we walked home, he scolded me with things like "Don't ever go after the cows without permission" and "Stay within sight of the house at all times." He told me that he found me because the cows came home in the middle of the day and Shep was with them. But they couldn't find me. So he followed the cow tracks through the woods.

Mom worked alongside Dad when she wasn't doing laundry by hand with a washboard and hanging the clothes on the line, trying to cook, clean, and keep up with an unfinished house while keeping an eye on me. Perhaps I was her biggest challenge. A spoiled child, I was always looking for attention or getting into something. I was curious about everything. I remember Mom heating water on the wood cookstove and scrubbing clothes in the kitchen sink with the washboard and a bar of yellow soap. Then taking them out to hang on the line, a thin rope strung between two trees, to dry. I liked to hang on the line and swing. Mom would yell at me. "Stop that. You are stretching out the line."

I would reply, "But it's fun." She told my dad that she didn't know what to do about it because I wouldn't stop. So Daddy made me a rope swing in a tree near the house. He even cut notches in the ends of a short board for the rope to fit in so I had a good seat to sit on. If Mom had a few minutes, she would go outside with me and push me on the rope swing. Poor Mom, I don't think I gave her any peace except when I was following Dad around. I soon learned to swing myself and spent hours swinging and dreaming I could fly like the birds.

Normally, I was a happy child and had my parents all to myself. I had a swing to daydream on and Shep to keep me company. *What more did I need?* Sticks make great boats in the mud puddles after a rain. I got to help Mom and Dad. I could make mud pies. I pretty much had the run of the eighty acres. Just so I could see the house and didn't go beyond the barbed wire or stump fence that Dad had up around the farm. Who would want to? Those barbs were wicked, and getting beyond the mazes of stumps was impossible.

So many memories. Dad was a dedicated farmer and had purchased the eighty acres to make a living farming for his family. Most of the land had to be cleared of trees, stumps, and brush in order to farm it. We had no shortage of firewood. My favorite part of the farm was the creek running through it, but I couldn't see the house from there, even though I could just follow the old railroad bed that was the driveway and trail through the farm. The train tracks had been removed, so it made a good solid road. Dad did have to replace the bridge so we could cross the creek.

Not only did Dad work hard to get our farm going, he helped Grandma on their farm about four miles away. Grandpa had fallen and broke his back, so of course, he was unable to do farmwork. I especially remember one day, Mom and Dad were out in a field on my grandparents' farm loading up the hay wagon. I vaguely remember horses pulling the wagon. I was supposed to go to town with Grandma. My uncle was going to take us with his new car. It had a rumble seat. I decided I didn't want to go to town with Grandma. I didn't remember riding in a car before and sitting in the rumble seat looked scary.

I told Mom and Dad, "I am not going with Grandma."

After a bit of an argument, Mom said, "Okay, but you have to go to the house and tell Grandma that you are not going."

So I went to the house and told Grandma.

She wouldn't hear of it. She picked up a stick and sternly said, "I told your mom I would take you to town. You are going with me."

So I did.

While we were gone, Mom and Dad came to the barn with the hay. They expected to see me but didn't. Now I did it again. This time, it was not my plan to be lost. But Mom and Dad looked everywhere including digging through the hay pile in the barn. I will never forget the look of relief on Mom's face and the scolding I got when we got back from town. I don't remember the trip to town.

Not long after that, my uncle went into the Army. Dad borrowed his car for us to use while he was gone. So we were now motorized. Never to return. About that time, Dad collected used parts and made a tractor. He called it the doodle bug. No more horses ever. Dad was ready to be done with horses. They would get cranky and not cooperate. They would get sick and have to be doctored, and they had to be fed and watered.

2

When I was old enough, Grandma B. encouraged my parents to take me to Sunday school to learn about God. Mom seemed reluctant, but she took me anyhow. She fretted that I didn't have any Sunday clothes. She did starch and iron my best play dress, I think it was light blue, and she polished my only pair of shoes. Those brown leather oxfords shined up pretty good. I remember walking into the basement of the church hanging on to her hand.

I asked her, "What are we going to do here?"

She said, "Here is where you get to learn about God. I will come back to get you in a little while, when it is done."

We walked down a dark hallway. I was scared and sure we were going to the wrong place. We rounded the corner into a bright sunny room. I saw a couple small round tables with maybe three or four children my size sitting at one of the tables and a woman standing near them. Mom told me that the woman was the teacher and I should listen to her.

The teacher noticed us right away and talked to my mom. Then said, as she placed a coloring page on the table and pulled out a little chair, "Mary, you may sit in this chair and color this page. The others have already started."

The coloring page was of a man in a long robe holding a lamb. She then started to talk about Jesus. Something about, "Jesus is the Good Shepherd, he takes care of the lambs."

I thought, *I am here to learn about God.* I stood up, put my hands on my hips, and defiantly said, "Who's Jesus anyway?"

The teacher looked a bit shocked, then quietly explained that Jesus is God or God's son. I was then happy and sat down to color and listen. That was my first memory of Jesus. We sang "Jesus Loves Me." By then, I couldn't wait to know more about this Jesus and wanted to go to Sunday school every week. We didn't always go to church and Sunday school because we were eight miles out of town and had cows and chickens that needed to be taken care of or the weather was bad. It was hard to get there sometimes.

Mother was constantly busy, so whenever possible, I got to help Daddy. I became Daddy's girl. Could it be that I became a little spoiled? One of my favorite memories was taking my tin cup out to the barnyard while Daddy was milking the cows in the evening. He would fill it with milk directly from the cow. Nothing tasted better than warm fresh milk at bedtime. He even taught me to milk the cow myself. I was not too sure. I liked doing it, but the cow didn't seem too happy to have an amateur messing with her. She wiggled around and mooed. Sometimes Dad would give me a bucket of chicken feed and let me throw it out to the chickens one handful at a time, while he filled their water buckets and feed hoppers. It was fun to have the chickens run to me like I was really important.

It was a great day when we got an icebox. It was like a refrigerator, but the freezer on top held a block of ice. I remember the ice man bringing a huge (to me) block of ice, a bit smaller than a hay bale, for the icebox to keep things cold. He carried it with scary round tongs big enough to pick up a kid. Dad told me that they cut the ice from the lake in winter and stored it in a big warehouse until summer. We couldn't keep ice cream in the icebox, but it kept meat and whatever we needed to keep cold for several days.

One day, the ice in the icebox melted before Mom had a chance to empty the drip pan underneath. She had a big puddle on the floor and was not happy that she had to clean it up. I heard her mumbling, "I should have emptied this earlier, then I wouldn't have to clean it up."

Once when we went shopping, we brought home a quart of ice cream. We had to eat it all right away because it would melt. I thought it was too cold, so I put my dish on the stove to heat it. Mom and Dad had a good laugh that day.

Occasionally, my cousins came over. A couple of them were my age, so we loved to play together. We played outside whenever the weather permitted. They seemed to think I lived in paradise or a wonderland. We had lots of places to hide when playing hide and seek. I thought it great that they were so curious about the farm. I would show them around like a tour guide. Much to my parents' dismay, my cousins didn't know we were not supposed to chase the chickens or that the hay could cave in and cover them. We usually ended up arguing over who would swing in *my* swing. The creek was forbidden territory unless an adult was with us. So I just never took them that far from the house. I liked it when my cousins came over.

Also, I loved when we went to their house because they had different stuff, like books to look at and more toys. Plus another cousin lived just around the corner. Even better, Grandma W. lived across the road from them. She had cookies and listened to our chatter. Grandma W. even had an indoor bathroom and a closet with a big toy box full of toys.

Aunt Mary lived with Grandma and Grandpa. She was a teenager and fun. She played with us, took our pictures with her camera, and played records on her windup Victrola. One of my favorites was "The Little Engine That Could." Even after I got home, I would be singing, "I think I can, I think I can."

Grandma kept the cookies in the lower cupboard near the sink. Once I went to sneak a cookie. Grandpa caught me. I got a severe scolding. After that, I was afraid of Grandpa and didn't dare to get cookies without permission.

Going to either of my Grandmas' houses was fun for me. Especially when cousins were there. One evening, we were having a good time at Grandma B.'s, my dad decided we had to go home because he had to milk the cows and feed the animals. I didn't want to go. They tried dragging me, but I laid down on the floor and started kicking and yelling, "I don't want to go." They tried to calm me and get me to go, but I wasn't having anything to do with it.

Finally, Dad said, "I guess we will just have to leave her here."

They won't do that, they will just stay longer, I thought.

As they started out the door, I jumped up and ran after them, crying all the way. So much for getting my way that time.

About the same age, I was old enough to help my dad get the eggs. He gave me a small basket to put them in. I thought I was Daddy's big helper, until one of the chickens was sitting on a nest. Not knowing how to get her off so I could get the eggs, I told Dad, "That chicken won't get off the nest so I can get the eggs." He showed me to just reach under her and feel around. Another chicken was on a nest, so I tried what Dad showed me. That chicken pecked my hand, and it hurt. It was a long time after that until I tried to take the eggs out from under a chicken.

Holidays were pure excitement to me. Once I got a windup train with pieces of tracks. The train had an engine that pulled two cars, one was a caboose. I didn't know what the tracks were. They looked like broken wires to me. So Mother showed me how to put them together. Then they were in a circle maybe three feet across. Mom showed me how to wind up the train and put it on the tracks. Sometimes when just the engine was on the tracks and was going fast, it would jump off the track because the circle was so small and it would go too fast. I soon learned that if it was hooked to the cars and went slower, it stayed on the tracks. It was hard to get them hooked together after winding the engine.

Once I got square building blocks with letters, numbers, and colors on them. I loved to build steeples and see how tall I could get it before it fell down. Someone, Grandma's I think, made rag dolls. The girl in me enjoyed playing with them, but I think I liked the train better. Most holidays, we went to one of the Grandmas for a huge dinner with turkey and apple pie for desert. Cousins were there to play with.

Once in a while, on snowy days, Mother made time to go outside and make a snowman with me or showed me how to make and throw snowballs. That usually didn't last too long because I would get cold.

My cousins had a small narrow metal runner sled. I wanted one too. We had a tiny hill near our house. That was all I needed. So for Christmas, my dad made me a big wooden sled with homemade metal runners. Ungrateful child that I was, I stamped my feet and said, "I wanted one like my cousins." I don't know how or where, but my dad came up with one a short time later. He ended up using the big one to haul wood for the woodstove.

One Easter, I was told I had an Easter basket from the Easter bunny, but he hid it. After crying because I didn't know where to look for it, Mom took me to the entrance shed. Next to the wood pile, she showed me a big farm bushel basket with straw and maybe a dozen brightly colored eggs. It was a dumb farm basket and chicken eggs. I didn't want that either, it wasn't like the ones in the stores.

One night, there was a terrible loud buzzing sound that seemed to be just outside the window. I cried and would not be consoled because it scared me. I did not know what it was. Dad went outside in the dark and found the little thing. He brought in a cicada and showed me it was simply a noisy grasshopper. After that, I always wanted to know what any noises were before I got scared.

One day, a very official looking man in a uniform drove into our yard. Dad and I were outside. I heard the man say something like, "You have to register or I have to take you with me."

I remember the fear that he would take my daddy away. I ran into the house crying to Mother, "He's going to take my daddy away." Come to find out, Daddy didn't know he had to register for the draft. He had thought that because he was a farmer, he was exempt. Yes, he was exempt, but he didn't know he still had to register. He promptly registered. My daddy didn't have to go away.

I realized we were different from other people when my parents were going to a wedding and got a babysitter for me. Dad showed the babysitter how to work the kerosene lantern and said he was sorry we didn't have electricity like they did. She was okay with it and that they used to have one like that. I started to wonder, *What is electricity and why don't we have it?* I found out we were on a side road and the power lines hadn't gone through yet.

Not too long after that, I remember a man hanging something from the ceiling. I would soon learn it was a bare lightbulb. He showed my parents how to turn on the light with the switch that was on the receptacle that the bulb was turned into. Let there be light. Wow we were now up with most of the people in town. Watch us go. Soon we had an electric washing machine. Mom still had to turn the handle on the rollers for the wringer.

One day in June, my mother went away for a few days. I stayed at Grandma's. Mom came home with a crying wetting bundle. It looked like a baby doll, but it wiggled and had to be fed. I wasn't sure I liked it. They called her Judy, and she took the attention I thought was mine.

Very soon on a nice day, my Grandmother W., some of my aunts, and cousins came for a visit. No one paid any attention to me. They brought presents for the baby and spent most of the time fussing over her. Finally, I couldn't take it anymore. I put my hands on my hips and yelled in a most angry voice, "What did you bring her home for?"

Everyone looked surprised and shocked. I felt embarrassed and angry when I started to realize I wasn't as important as I thought. I may have been jealous of her forever after that.

I played with my cousins when they came over. Another time, I enjoyed other kids is when I was invited to Bible school. Bible school was the best. I loved to sing the songs and learn about Jesus. One day, one of the teachers showed us some bibles. She said the little red ones were free, it was the Gideon's New Testament, but if we wanted the whole Bible, we had to buy it. I wanted the whole Bible, so I went home and told my mom. We were poor. Just barely surviving, and Mom said we couldn't buy anything extra. I begged, "But I need the whole Bible. I need to learn everything about God."

Mom argued, "Why do you need it, you can't even read?"

I replied, "You said that I am going to school to learn how to read soon."

She finally said, "You have some money in your piggy bank. If you have enough in there, you may buy one."

I shook the coins out through the hole in the bottom. Mom didn't think there was enough, but the next day, I took them anyway. I gave them to the teacher. She talked to the other teachers and said that it was enough. I don't think it really was, but they let me have a small Bible. Today I still have that Bible. My mom saved it for me.

3

That same year, my whole life changed. Mom took me to school on an early September morning. I remember the one-room schoolhouse with eight grades for one teacher. That first day, before we went inside, I noticed some boys came on their horses. I wanted to ride a horse to school, but we didn't have a horse anymore and girls couldn't ride them because they had to wear skirts to school. Some of the older girls were playing hopscotch on a shape they had drawn on the dirt.

Mom said, "See, you will have other kids to play with."

I was not impressed. I was just scared that Mom was trying to get me out of the way and that baby would get all Mom's attention.

When we got inside the school, Mom showed me the girls' coatroom where I could hang my coat and put my lunch. Then I saw one big room with a bunch of little tables for one person each. They called them desks. I was surprised to see that they had shelf-like spaces under the tops to put stuff like books, paper, and pencils in. The desks had a round hole on the top right. They called it an ink well for a little bottle of ink. The teacher assigned one of the eighth-grade boys to show me around. I sat with him until she found a desk for me.

Soon the teacher had one of the older boys ring a bell. The bell was in the tower over the school and had a rope hanging down just inside the door. You had to be tall to reach the rope. When all the kids were inside, she got in front of the room and started telling everyone to sit down and be quiet. The room became quiet. Then she told us to stand up, put our hand on our heart, and say the pledge of allegiance to the flag. I couldn't find my heart, so the boy next to me showed me to just put my hand on my chest like he did. Then we sang a couple songs. I felt dumb because I didn't know the words to anything. I learned, "Bell bottom trousers coat of navy blue, I love a sailor boy, and he loves me too." I learned the words but had no clue what they meant.

Soon I had to go to the bathroom or outhouse. I tried to tell the teacher.

She said, "If you want to talk, you need to raise your hand, then I will call on you."

I did raise my hand, but it was too late. She had one of the older girls take me to the outhouse. We didn't have dry pants, so I was sent home early. I had to walk one and a half miles home on a narrow gravel road by myself. Mother had shown me the way, so I wasn't scared. I just hurried home to get dry clothes.

Other days, I might stop along the way to pick wildflowers or watch the animals and birds. Mom acted like she didn't like that I was late. It didn't seem to register with me until she said that she worried about me. She said that she worried that a wild animal got me or someone stole me or I got hurt and couldn't get home. She said that she wanted to come looking for me, but she couldn't carry my baby sister all over. Finally, I got the message and started hurrying home. Even so, that was another indication to me that that baby sister was more important than me. I hurried home without stopping along the way because I didn't want Mother upset with me.

I told one of the girls, "I have to hurry home because my mom worries."

The girl said, "I know a way you can get home a little quicker. Come with me after school."

So I went with her after school. It turned out to be a shortcut through the woods. She lived about halfway down the path and stopped there but told me, "Keep following the path and you will come to the road you usually take. It's like we are cutting off the corner to make it quicker."

The problem then, it was tempting to stop to play at her house.

In school another time, the boy next to me started to talk to me. I told him we had to be quiet. By then, we were both in trouble. Teacher took us one at a time into the coatroom and wrapped on our knuckles with a ruler. Just another reason for me to think school was not good. *After all, it wasn't even my fault.*

Occasionally, my parents didn't think they would be home when I got there, so they would make arrangements with the neighbor lady, just around the corner, and tell me to stop there on the way home. She was a bit chunky but had the prettiest smile and the best cookies. I think sometimes I even took naps there until my parents came for me. Once they hadn't told me to stop at her house. I got home and no one was there. So I walked back about a quarter mile to the corner where we turned to our house. I didn't think I should go back to the nice lady's house because then Mom and Dad wouldn't see me. So I sat on the side of the road to wait for them. No cars went by. It was a little traveled narrow road. It seemed like forever until they finally came. Surely they must have deserted me. When they finally came, I was crying. They said they were sorry that they hadn't planned to be so long.

Sometimes I argued with Mom. I remember arguing with my mom a couple times.

"Eat your oatmeal, you can't go to school on an empty stomach."

"I can't. It makes me want to throw up."

"You will eat your oatmeal or I will feed you."

So I tried. Yup, I vomited right there. Not sure of the outcome from there.

Another time we argued. "Mom, don't, it hurts," I said as mother was brushing my long hair and about to braid it. Swatting at her and trying to pull her hand away, trying to fight her off, I yelled, "No, no, I won't let you." Swat… went the hairbrush to my butt. The handle broke and the brush end went flying. Mother still had the handle in her hand. Inside, I laughed. I thought I had won. In the end, I got a haircut.

The worst day started out as the best day. I had just learned to read. Suddenly, it seemed like a light went on.

Everything on the page started to make sense. I had read *Dick and Jane* from cover to cover and raised my hand to tell the teacher I could read it. When I looked around, no one was there. I looked everywhere, in the coatrooms. *Maybe they were all hiding. The woodshed attached to the back of the school is kind of dirty. They wouldn't want to hide there. Maybe they were outside for recess.* I looked all around outside, even in the outhouse. I knocked on the boys' outhouse door, but no one answered. I couldn't find anyone. A strange smell was in the air, and the whole sky was gray all the way to the ground. Like a gray fog. My eyes started to burn. It seemed like it was getting dark. *Maybe it's the end of the day and I missed the teacher sending us home.* I thought, *I better get home before it's night.* So I took the shortcut through the woods. It was so dark I could barely see the path, and the smell was terrible. I just knew the bears and wolves would get me before I saw them. My nose and eyes burned. By the time I got to the road, it was dark as night. My eyes were watering and burning. The wind was blowing hard. It was hard to walk straight, and the tiny stones on the gravel road blew and hit my bare legs, making it feel like they were being sandblasted or stung with hundreds of bees. I started to cry. I remember thinking, *I can't even see the road, but if I stick to the side here by the weeds, I should be okay. I could walk in the ditch, but there might be snakes.* So crying, I hurried toward home following the side of the road. I was about halfway when I saw car lights through the blackness. I was afraid it might be a stranger and thought to hide in the ditch. Not sure of what or who was coming or what was in the ditch, I kept stumbling along. The car stopped. I couldn't see the driver. I wanted to run.

A voice said, "What are you doing here?" It was my dad.

I just cried harder. He said, "Get in. I'll take you home."

I wasn't even sure how to get in the car because I couldn't see from the dark and crying. He reached out and helped me in the car, then took me home. He had to go back to help fight the forest fire. He was a volunteer firefighter. Mom calmed me, and I think I went to sleep.

When we went back to school, the teacher scolded me for leaving the building. She and the other kids had gone to see the fire and left me behind. *I got in trouble, but she is the one who left this little kid in school by herself.*

After that, I could never get 100 percent lost in my studies as one ear was always open in case I missed something important like another fire. I think I didn't even try to read after that or couldn't remember how. I had trouble trusting the great big world out there. Home is where I felt safe.

One day, I got home from school. Mom said, "Don't mess up your dress, we have to go to town to the doctor to look at baby for her checkup. Hurry, we don't have much time."

I protested. "But I have to say hi to Daddy."

Mom said, "Okay, but be quick. He is out by the barn unloading hay."

By now Dad had built the tractor out of used parts and used it instead of horses. I got there, and he was showing my older boy cousin what to do.

He said, "Just pull back on this rope after I stop. That will trip the fork to dump the hay on the pile and bring it down for another load." The fork that took the hay to the top of the big hay pile or stack was hooked to a rope that went through large pulleys in a couple trees and down the tree where we were and through a pulley at the bottom where they pulled the rope to take up the slack and bring the fork back down.

Dad went to the back, and I don't know where my cousin was, but I thought, *I am Daddy's big helper, I can do this*. As the tractor started moving, the rope started sliding through the lower pulley. *Okay, I will help*. I started pulling the rope. I couldn't stop it. I hung on for all I was worth. It pulled me closer and my hand ended up in the pulley with the rope whizzing past and ripping the flesh off my left index finger. In an attempt to get my hand out, I also hurt one finger on my other hand. Finally, I got my hand out. With both hands bleeding, I wrapped them in the skirt of my dress and ran to the house.

My mother was getting my little sister ready. She heard me crying and saw my hands in my dress. She said something like, "What did you do, get your dress all dirty?" When she saw my hand, I wonder to this day if she came close to fainting. One could see the bone all the way up my left index finger. The other hand had a burn on one finger and was bleeding. Mom cleaned me up as best she could in a hurry. Good thing we had borrowed my uncle's car. At the doctor's, he cleaned me up and wrapped my hands thick with bandages. It seems like the doctor said something like he wasn't sure what to do. We would just have to let it heal and be sure it didn't get infected and then decide.

The fingers healed with bone still showing through, and the index finger was so badly contracted, I couldn't unbend it. When the doctor saw it, he said that we could either cut it off or there was a new doctor in Grand Rapids. He was doing some experiments in plastic surgery and the crippled children's fund would help with the expenses. So I spent many days at Blodgett Hospital in Grand Rapids.

The hospital was big and scary. My first memory was me being pushed on a gurney, saying, "I want my Mama." People pushing me assured me I was okay. They put me on a table in a weird-looking room. And put a mask over my face and told me to take some deep breaths. How could I? The smell was awful. Thankfully, I quickly fell asleep, so I didn't have to smell it. When I woke up, I was in a body cast with my left arm inside of it up against my side. I was told that was so I wouldn't move my hand and mess up their work. Eventually, I understood that a flap of skin had been loosed from my side but was still attached and they had sewn it to my finger to make new skin for my finger. In time, it would grow on my finger, and they could remove the skin from my side and finish sewing it to my finger. Then I wouldn't need the cast anymore.

I was not a happy camper in the hospital. I learned to stand up in the youth crib they had me in. I would stand there and yell and cry. Other children in the ward didn't seem to give them trouble like I did. Anyway, I remember one day, when I was being difficult during naptime. I didn't want to take a nap and made noise to let everyone know my feelings. After several warnings, the nurses wheeled my crib into the utility room and shut the door so I wouldn't keep the others awake. I remember standing up in that crib and spitting on everything I could in protest, along with the yelling. No one paid any attention to me. I seem to remember a nurse coming in after I quieted down and telling me she could take me back if I promised not to yell anymore.

My mom had gotten a job in Grand Rapids in order to be close by and have a little money. While I was in the hospital, she stayed with an aunt who lived in Grand Rapids.

On the good side, I was at the hospital over Christmas. People felt sorry for me, so I got lots of attention and gifts. One of my aunts and Grandma W. came. Grandma brought me a book. *Cinderella* became my favorite story. My Aunt Mary, who was about sixteen at the time, had made me a doll cradle out of a round oatmeal box. In it was a little baby doll in a sweet pale pink little night dress. My aunt had covered the entire box with pretty pink printed fabric and lace. The doll was covered with a handmade doll quilt. All were just the right size for the oatmeal box.

In and out of the hospital and six surgeries later, I could use my finger, and today at eighty-one years old, it still functions very well. Only problem is it gets cold easily. The circulation is not as good as the others. Growing up, I hid the scar so people wouldn't notice. People maybe thought that I was so good to fold my hands right over left all the time, but really all I was doing was hiding the scar. I think the only one who really noticed was me. I still have a scar on my hand and on my side where the skin was removed.

Since then, doctors have learned to slice skin to remove it so it can be totally removed and placed where needed without a cast. I learned that after the doctor experimented on me, he started doing face lifts and did the face lift of one of my favorite movie stars.

4

Returning to school after that was not easy. I cried at everything. The mean boys figured that out. I had to walk home with four brothers. They teased and tormented me. They called me "Mary, Mary, quite contrary, how does your garden grow?" Or Mary had a little lamb. They would repeat the whole rhymes to me until I cried hard. My mom made the best baked beans for the potlucks. So they started calling me bean blower. One of them my age was so mean, he knew my hand got extra cold so he took my mittens, then went to the top of a neighbor's silo and left them there. I cried. It was my only pair of mittens. His brother, a year older, felt sorry for me and went up and brought my mittens down.

Walking with the boys went from bad to worse as spring came. One day, instead of two of the boys turning to go toward their home, they turned with me to go the opposite way toward my home. It was less than a quarter of a mile to my house. There was a dense woods between the corner and my drive way. The one that took my mittens and his biggest brother said that they wanted to show me something in the woods. I didn't think I should go, but they persisted. We were just in the woods a short way when I said, "Where is it?"

The younger boy, my age, said, "Here," as he was taking his boy part out of his pants. The older bigger boy was trying to pull my panties down. I started yelling. They wrestled me to the ground. I kept yelling until the bigger one put his hand over my mouth while the other one got on top of me and started trying to rape me. The bigger one coached the smaller one what to do. When I realized what they were trying to do, I squeezed my legs together as hard as I could with everything I had, but the kid had his thing between them. I think he thought he was successful. However, about then, I heard my Dad's tractor coming out of the driveway. The boys did too. They took off running. Dad said that he came because he heard me yelling. Dad took me home to Mother. After trying to get me to tell them what happened, he took the tractor, I assume, to talk to the boys' parents. After that, I didn't have to walk with those mean boys anymore. If I remember correctly, the teacher let me out a bit early and told me to go straight home so the boys couldn't catch me.

In those early years, I didn't have many friends. The closest neighbors my age were a mile away. They lived right where one would pass their house when taking the shortcut path to school. I remember they had a nice older boy and three girls. I seldom stopped to play because I had to hurry home so the bad boys didn't catch me. I do remember another girl named Barbara a few miles away. Mother took me to her house to play a couple times when I was maybe in second grade.

I did play with my cousins when they came over every few weeks. Another time I enjoyed other kids is when I was invited to Bible school. It was held about a mile and a quarter from my house on the corner I had to pass if I didn't take the shortcut to school. So I could walk there. The bad boys didn't go to Bible school.

One summer, when I was about seven, after Bible school, we went to Grandma's to help them because Grandpa was ill. I asked if I could go out and climb the apple trees. It was one of my favorite things to do. In Bible school, we had learned to sing, "I have the joy, joy, joy down in my heart, I have the peace that passes understanding down in my heart, and I have the love of Jesus down in my heart." Also I had learned that we could talk to Jesus any time. As I walked the path to the apple orchard, I told Him, *I sure would like to have the joy and peace and love.* How I said it, I don't know, but I believe He has been with me ever since.

With two children and another one expected, Dad added a bedroom to our little house. I slept in the new room, and as soon as my sister was old enough, she would join me. There was a curtain for a door. I remember at Christmas, lying on my belly, peeking under the curtain, waiting for Santa Claus. How could I miss him? The tree was right there next to the door. The next morning, I woke up in my bed. I had missed Santa. When I got up to check the Christmas tree, there was a very large rag doll sitting there. I think she was bigger than me. Later I learned that my Grandma B. had made it for me. The doll had a printed dress with a white pinafore apron, bloomers for underpants, and yellow yarn hair. Buttons for eyes.

As a young child, I had dreams. In the worst one, there was a huge, maybe ten feet tall, bear-like monster that was beating me with a club. As I look back, it never hurt, but I was horribly scared anyway. I would wake up crying, and Mom or Dad would try to calm me. They wanted to know why I was crying. I couldn't tell them. I had no word for monster or dream. All I did was cry. They would try to comfort me. I think sometimes I fell asleep in their arms. Thinking back, I wonder if God was already showing me that big scary things would happen in my life, but they never would really hurt me.

We had a rather unique driveway. It was raised higher than the ground level. I was told it was an old railroad track bed from the early train that went from Grand Rapids to Grand Haven. The rails had been removed. Once in a while, Dad found a big rusty square spike they had left behind. The drive went through the entire length of our eighty acres to across the road on to near where my school was, in a village they called Podunk that was no longer there. What happened to the village? I don't know. I was told that at one time, the train stopped there to take people to Grand Rapids.

So many happy memories living there, including our dog Shep and a barn cat I became attached to. I spent numerous hours swinging and dreaming in the swing Daddy made and felt honored when Mother took a break from her chores and went outside to push me on the swing or, in winter, to build a snowman with me. Dad didn't do much with me after I hurt my hand. Perhaps he thought I would get hurt again.

Sometimes I was assigned to watch my baby sister. It was okay unless I felt like I was missing something, like the day we went out to the back field to pick strawberries. I wanted to pick strawberries too. We went in the car. Dad parked the car under a shade tree. Sister was sleeping on the seat. I was to stay in the car, watch her, and call them if she woke up. I had one of my fits but ended up staying there.

Another time, Mom and Dad went to a dance at the township hall. They parked so I could see people dancing through a window. The window was open so I could hear the music. It was a warm summer evening. I wanted to go inside and see what I could see, but my sister was sleeping on the car seat, so I was told to stay in the car but if my sister woke up to come and get them. I was not happy. After I saw my parents dance past the window, I believe I went to sleep too. In those days, that was not thought of as bad. We were out in the country where safety was not a concern.

5

I was nearly eight when my second baby sister, Betty, was born. In spite of the room Dad had added on, that winter over Christmas break, we moved in with my grandparents who lived about five miles away. I remember at first I slept in the dining room behind a door on an army cot. The woodstove would keep me warm there. Grandma and Grandpa had a bedroom on the main floor. Mom and Dad slept up the stairs in the first room where the heat from the woodstove would go up. I do not remember where my sisters slept.

I do remember the living room was called the parlor and had a curtain closing it off from the rest of the house. It was off limits to kids. In it was a large glassed-in bookcase filled with books and a pump organ that one could pump the pedals and press the keys to get great sounds. Also the usual furnishings for a living room, including a burgundy couch plus a wall-to-wall rug with a burgundy design. Only special guests were allowed in the parlor.

At Christmas, Grandma put up a Christmas tree in the parlor with real candles that were lit for a very short time on Christmas Eve. Kids could go in the parlor and watch. I was amazed by the angel hair Grandma had spread all over the tree. I had never seen such tiny threads of white silky, very wide ribbons. The next year, electric lights were on the tree. If a bulb came loose or went out, all the other lights went out too.

One day, I snuck into the parlor because I wanted to see what the books in the case were. I was beginning to learn to read. I found a book that was a different language than English. I wanted to know what it said. I took it into the kitchen and told Mom, "I can't read this."

Grandma was there. She said, "Where did you get that?"

I told her. Oh my, did I ever get in trouble. I don't think I had ever seen Grandma so mad. Was it because I was in the parlor or because I asked about the book? I did find out the book had come from the "Old Country," when Grandma was ten and their family moved here.

I am not sure why we moved in with Grandma and Grandpa. Was it because we were having trouble keeping warm where we were or because my Grandpa had fallen and hurt his back and also was going blind with glaucoma? Dad could run the farm because Grandma couldn't do it all and take care of Grandpa too.

It started another chapter in my life. A couple neighbor girls lived just across the field. They had fun things like a balance scale in the barn where we weighed ourselves, wishing we were up to one hundred pounds. They had a hammock they said that their dad had used in the Navy, and geese. I didn't much like the geese because I thought they would peck me. I liked their lawn swing where we all could sit at once and talk and swing. The girls also taught me how to make little purses with big leaves. One time, one of the girls shocked me because she had a garden snake wrapped around the handlebars of her bike.

Grandma taught me how to make hollyhock dolls. I could make lots of beautiful dancing girls with full pretty skirts by turning the flower upside down and peeling the green off the back of the flower. Grandma grew pretty flowers everywhere. The daffodils were so pretty, the Spirea bushes bloomed white, and the lilacs surrounded the outhouse and covered up the aroma when they were in bloom. The swing Dad made was bigger in a really big tree. Even so, I was sad because both my cat and dog, Shep, disappeared shortly after we moved.

In spring the ditches had pollywogs in them. I loved to wade in the water and catch them. Sometimes I would take my dad's boots and try not to get my feet wet. But I usually did get the inside of the boots wet. Dad was not happy, but he did show me how to wad up newspaper and put it inside the boots to soak up the water.

Sometimes I still had scary dreams, like the one where there were snakes writhing inside a mattress-sized open box. I would be so scared but never could understand why they never came out of the box. It kind of reminded me of the dream about the monster. It was like there was an invisible something that would not let the snakes out.

School there was not much better. I only had one quarter mile to walk, but it was still a one-room school with eight grades and more kids, about forty-four. The poor teacher had all she could do to maintain order. It must have been too much because we got a new teacher almost every semester. Not only did she have to teach and keep control of unruly kids, but she had to keep the furnace going with wood or maybe coal. She was the janitor and did some maintenance too.

The first day at school was not good. It was a bitter cold winter day. I had outgrown most of my clothes. Mother and Grandmother decided my coat was not heavy enough and I needed a sweater under it. The warm red one Mother had knit for me was too small. Grandma offered to let me wear one of hers. It was the ugliest gray old gold I had ever seen. The sleeves had to be rolled up, and the body was as long as my dress. I did have snow pants to wear. My response was, "I am not wearing that ugly sweater to school." No way was I wearing that ugly sweater to school. The argument I got was, "You have to go to school and you have to walk, so you have to be warm." They won and I hated that sweater.

At school, the girls had their own entrance to their coatroom, and the teacher even showed me the restroom. All there was was one single toilet which I had never seen before. Even though I could figure out how to sit on it, I didn't know about flushing it. The outhouse was still in back, but they weren't using it. The teacher acted like she didn't know what to do with me. So far, I couldn't read even though I did know some of my letters. I think I blocked out reading after my accident. Adding and subtracting were mysteries to me. I was supposed to be in third grade. It wasn't long until the teacher put me in with the second graders and in first-grade reading class. At least there, I could start to learn. My mom and dad tried to work with me to catch up. I remember crying over arithmetic. Once I figured out how to read, there was no stopping me. My mother encouraged that. At one point, she directed me to *Cheaper by the Dozen* from the church library. And the *Bobbsey Twins* series, which I devoured. *Cherry Ames Nurse* books were exciting for me, reminding me of my times in the hospital.

Fridays were my favorite days as we did arts and crafts. I was amazed when I learned how to make paper chains. And special Fridays, we had a magic show person come and pull rabbits out of the hat. He talked about Jesus. He even invited us to Bible school in the summer and said the bus would come for us. Once we had Edgar Bergan and Charlie McCarthy before they were famous. I couldn't believe a wooden dummy could talk. I finally wanted to learn everything, but the teacher didn't have just me. Some of the big kids learned that I cried easily, so teasing was an issue. An eighth-grade boy sat next to me for a time. He had a jackknife that he would get out when the teacher wasn't looking. He would barely touch my arm with the point and not break the skin. I would tell him to quit. The teacher would tell me to be quiet. When I told her he poked me with a knife, he had it hid, and she didn't believe me.

I was usually the last one chosen for games because I was slow and weak. Red Rover was the worst game because everyone knew I couldn't hang on when they came across. I was the weak link in the chain. The most fun was jumping the ditch with water in it, but we were not allowed to do it during school hours even though the ditch was alongside the school property. On our way home, more than once, I got my shoes and dress wet because I didn't make it across and fell in. One time, a couple girls and I walked behind the school and a bit beyond the fence. We heard a small rattlesnake, then saw it. I remembered my experience from before and made sure the other girls didn't go near. We didn't want to tell the teacher because we knew we were outside the schoolyard. But we told her anyway, and everyone had their recess cut short that day. The school had a bell. If kids were big enough and earned the right, they got to ring it to come in for recess. That day, the teacher had to ring it because we girls were too short, and she wanted the kids in immediately. I loved to swing on the swings, but there were only three or four swings and lots of kids to swing on them. We were encouraged to let the little kids on them or at least take turns, so we had to take turns while the older kids played ball or games.

The best thing I learned at that school was when I went to the teacher while she was feeding wood to the furnace fire during recess. I asked could I do something. Don't remember what it was. When she said no, I said, "But the other kids do."

She said, "If the other kids jumped into this fire, would you?"

That's when I learned that following the crowd was not always wise.

I made a friend named Nannette. She moved away before I got to know her very well. More about her later.

For my tenth or twelfth birthday, I got a bike. I had wished for a bike for a long time and saved money for one. Even prayed for one. That year, I put in my savings, which was half enough. My parents put in the rest. That big blue, brand-new bike was the joy of my life. It sure was hard to ride it on the gravel road, but I did anyway. One day, a car came up behind me. I didn't hear it. They honked its horn. Surprised and trying to hurry to get out of the way, I fell. Did I stop riding my bike to school after that?

When I got a bike, I was more independent. It was decided that I needed to learn to swim. We found out that the Red Cross had swimming lessons maybe four miles away on Stearns Bayou across from Felix's Marina. Once Mom got me enrolled and took me there a few times, I was allowed to ride my bike. I loved to swim and could hold my breath and stay underwater longer than anyone else. The teacher even warned me not to do it so long.

Once we sold seeds for March of Dimes and I earned a ruler. I was a success. Another success was sewing. I had been trying to sew doll clothes for a time, then my mother decided she could have me and some other girls to our house for 4-H sewing. I still remember the white dish towel and the pink apron I made from feed sack material. I was so proud. The second year, I made a skirt, and by the third year, I made blue pants with a zipper and a matching blue shirt with buttons and button holes. That year, I was runner-up for first place. The competition was tough, so I came in second.

My sister was five years younger and would go to kindergarten the next year. We got to take a younger sibling for a special day at school. It was snowing outside, and we had to walk home with the rest of the kids. I don't remember the others having siblings with them. On the way home, the other kids made a human chain across the road and said they wouldn't let me take my sister home. I was scared and felt responsible for her safety. I figured since we were up to our farm property and there was a barbed wire fence between us and the fields beside the road, with a pile of soft snow along the fence, I could get her home that way. *Okay, I will get her home. She is my responsibility. I will throw her over the fence, and she will land in the soft snow.* So I picked her up and threw her over the fence. She landed in the light fluffy snow on the other side. She didn't seem to be hurt, but she was covered with snow everywhere, face, eyes, and her clothes. She got up and took off running and crying to the house. I crawled through the fence and followed behind her. By the time I got there, she told Mom I threw her in the snow and I got in trouble. Somehow I was supposed to get beyond the kids, I guess. I never did figure how I was supposed to deal with the situation. To this day, I don't think my sister ever forgave me.

I still had scary dreams sometimes. One that kept recurring was I was walking home from school by myself when two county snowplow trucks came side by side behind me. I was afraid they would catch me and plow me over. I thought, *I can't even go to the side of the road to get out of their way.* In my dream, I ran as fast as I could and got home. No one was there but Grandma, rocking in her rocking chair. Short of breath, I tried to tell her that I was afraid they would come after me, but she never answered me. Was that another dream that my fears were unfounded and I would be okay? Or was it to help me later to know I was on my own and Grandma couldn't help me?

Dad taught me how to drive the truck and tractor. He would help put the truck in granny gear and showed me how to hold the clutch down. I would let it up after they loaded corn on to the back and push it down when Dad yelled stop so he could pick and load more corn. It was much the same with the tractor, moving from small hay pile to small hay pile while they used pitch forks to load the hay.

We had a small building that I adopted for a playhouse. I had found things around the farm to make it my retreat. I am not sure why, but Dad wanted it for something. Of course, I protested. So Dad's solution was to bring in some old lumber and set posts in the ground so I could make myself another playhouse. I had more fun nailing the boards to the posts, after Dad showed me how, than I ever did using the playhouse. I think I had outgrown playhouses about then.

The worst thing I remember is my mother and grandmother fighting in the middle of the kitchen. They were yelling and in a physical grip like they were wrestling. I stayed in to watch the little kids. My sister ran out and told our dad. He came in and yelled stop, but they didn't, so he pushed them apart. They both landed on the floor. Not long after that, Dad and my uncles built a little house on two acres of land on a hill near us. The house was maybe twenty-four feet by twenty-four feet. It had a living room-kitchen combination across the front and the back had a bedroom, bath, and utility. Not very big but it was all Grandma and Grandpa needed.

By then, our family had grown and two brothers had been added. I became the little kid watcher whenever Mom was busy. My favorite thing to do with the boys was dig with them in the ditch with yellow sand. It was their sandbox. We tried digging to China, but we never made it. We did, however, dig and found water.

We went to church most every Sunday. We had special church clothes that Mom had gotten for us either at Easter or Christmas. I thought the sermons were boring, but in front of the church was a painting of Jesus walking on water, holding Peter's hand. Most Sundays, I studied that picture wondering how Jesus could walk on water but Peter couldn't. The church had a big pipe organ, and the organist played like she loved it. I can still hear that loud rich music. I think people must have heard it blocks away. To this day, I love the music in church, but none can measure up to that.

Somewhere along the way, I learned that Christmas was the most special time. It was way more than presents and dinners. It became apparent the year we would make our usual trip to church on Christmas Eve where us kids always had a part to say in the traditional pageant. It was snowing hard. The windshield wipers on the car didn't work, and the car had no heat. Even so, Mom and Dad piled us all in the car. With our blankets, the little kids and I huddled together in the back seat. Dad had to stop along the way to clean off the windshield. How many times in that eight-mile drive, I don't recall. Mom in front was an extra set of eyes. We had to go to church. Was it tradition or what was expected of us? As I think back, maybe it was, because Dad knew that the birth of Jesus was the most important event in history. To hear him tell it, he was not the best in his younger years. Without the grace of God to send Jesus to pay the price for our misbehaviors, we would all be condemned to everlasting punishment.

6

More about school. The best thing that happened to me in sixth grade was the school board decided we were overcrowded and they would send the seventh- and eighth-grade kids to town for school. There was one problem: the junior high school in Grand Haven was already filled beyond capacity. But Spring Lake just across the river had room for us. So in my seventh and eighth and ninth grades, I went to Spring Lake Junior High. I finally learned something. The subjects were divided into separate classes. Miss Schroder and Miss VanBukering taught me how to write sentences and stories, read, and do book reports. I remember having to write a story about the future. I wrote that sidewalks would move and people would have helicopters in their garage. The roofs would open so the helicopters could just drop in. Cars would be very streamlined, almost like bullets. I never dreamed that we would have cell phones or computers; they were unheard of then. I was just getting used to a party line phone with the wires strung along the fence wherever they could; poles hadn't been put up. How Mr. VanWierin got me from E's in math in seventh grade to A's in algebra in ninth grade, I will never know. I do know he had the patience of Job and was a great motivator. Science was fun. I had the biggest bug collection in the class. I guess living on an eighty-acre farm was an advantage. Mr. Boyink was also the principal and taught science part-time. I wasn't much into geography or history, but I learned something there too. We had physical education once a week at the new elementary school several blocks away. A bus took us there, but we had to walk back to junior high. I guess that was part of the program. I was not good at any kind of sports, but I tried.

We could also get hot lunch by taking a bus to the elementary school and walking back. If we didn't get hot lunch, we ate our packed lunch in the junior high auditorium and then went outside. Phyllis was my best friend from my old school. After lunch, we would walk down town a couple blocks away and look around. Town was only two blocks long. Sometimes we would stop at the bakery and get a cookie or we would go to the drugstore and get a cherry coke and a *Hit Parade* magazine that had the words to songs, then walk down the sidewalk singing all the way. Phyllis knew the tunes better than me.

One day, we went into the drugstore. I saw a key chain that had a take-apart puzzle on it. Someone had taken the puzzle apart. I decided I would help and fix it. While I was trying to fix it, the owner saw me. He thought I was trying to steal it. We were banned from the store the rest of the year. So no more cherry cokes.

Riding the bus to junior high was fun. It was a great experience for this country girl. The bus was an old city bus, and the drivers were off-duty policemen who knew how to deal with rowdy kids. I thought it was great to cross the swing bridge. Sometimes we had to wait, and we could watch the bridge swing the road sideways to let boats through. The lift bridge hadn't been built yet. Sitting with my friend Phyllis and talking like only a couple teenage girls can made the ride seem short.

Once, the bus broke down on a seldom-used country road. We didn't have cell phones then, but I remember that we got another ride to school. Either the policeman had a walkie talkie or he walked to the nearest house and phoned. Anyway, it was cold outside, and the bus got colder.

In junior high, I got a good dose of Bible training. You see, it was traditional at our church to be confirmed at that age. That meant going to church every Saturday morning and paying attention to Bible lessons and memorizing the Lord's Prayer, the Apostles Creed, the Ten Commandments along with many other passages that were in the *Luther's Small Catechism*. I wanted to learn all I could and couldn't understand why some of the kids in the class didn't pay attention. Something inside me told me it was very important. With my own money, I even bought a new Bible. I wanted one with a zipper on it so it would stay together better. I wanted to read it in bed, but Mother would see the light still on and yell up the stairs for me to turn out the light.

About then, we were entering the up-to-date world. We were excited to have a freezer. Dad butchered our own meat, beef, pork, and chicken. It was so much easier to preserve in a freezer than the canning and smoking they had to do before. Mom also froze vegetables and fruit. Strawberries were my favorite. We also got a TV. Who would think one could get pictures with people talking out of the air? Mother must have liked it on Saturdays because we would hurry to get our rooms cleaned so we could watch *The Big Top*. It was a real circus right in our living room.

We got a party line phone installed beside a doorway from the dining room to the kitchen. I think there were eight homes to a line. Someone was always on the line or wanted it. I was afraid of it in a rainstorm after one stormy day; I was walking through the door to the next room. Lightning cracked extremely loud. Less than two feet in front of me, a streak of lightning shot out of the handset of the phone. For years, I wondered why I didn't like to talk on the phone. One day, I remembered that incident and think my unconscious remembers.

My first experience dating was a double date where we met at the football games. So it wasn't really a date. My friend Phyllis liked a boy. They had met at the football games. His friend always tagged along. She encouraged me to come to the game with her and sit with Steve. I had no way to get there, but she came with her older brother who could drive, and I lived along the way, so they picked me up. Steve was a very nice kid. We sat together at the games and even held hands a couple times. Phyllis and her boyfriend would sneak off sometimes. I really loved the half times with the bands and the music, and I liked yelling with the cheerleaders. When the game ended, Phyllis and I would walk the few blocks to the drugstore on Washington

Street and wait for her brother who would pick us up there and bring us home.

Phyllis moved away after eighth grade, so in ninth grade, I was on my own. Going back to school in the fall of ninth grade, I was accused of bleaching my hair. After a summer of helping my dad in the fields, he paid me, and picking blueberries for a blueberry grower a couple miles away, my hair truly was sun-bleached. I am not sure the kids believed it was from the sun, but it got me a lot of attention. Most city kids didn't have the opportunity to be outside all day every day. So what did they know? Even so, I had earned enough money to buy my own school clothes. And I didn't have to bleach my hair to change the color.

Sometimes I went to the farmers market in Muskegon with my dad. It was fun to wait on customers. I loved it when it slowed down in the afternoon and I could walk down town and do my own shopping. Mother was not there to tell me what to get. I was careful with my money and mostly spent it on school clothes.

A short rabbit trail here. Muskegon Farmers Market had a variety of people. Being raised around white people, I couldn't understand why some people had dark skin, so one day, I asked my dad, "How come some people have brown skin?"

His reply, "Some people have different color skin, but they are all the same inside. Most people are good, and once in a while, people are bad. It doesn't matter if they are dark or light. Think about our cows. Some are spotted white, some are brown. They all give milk, and we don't think of them as different."

Dad didn't treat anyone different, nor did he complain about them because of color. That settled it for me.

Back to school. In school, I tried choir one year. All it did was convince me I could not sing. I think I am Mary one note. One day, the choir teacher kept us after school. We were the last class of the day in the elementary school music room. As a result, I missed my bus to go home, so I went to the office and borrowed a phone, then walked to town and waited. My poor mother had to come all that way, about twelve miles, to get me. After that, I think I skipped choir.

I made friends at the school and had forever school friends. Not the kind you stayed with at sleepovers, but friends at school. One girl Nannette had gone to my elementary school but had moved to Spring Lake a few years before. She invited me to her house a couple times for lunch, and we got to know each other better. I liked looking at the scrapbook she made with her dream house in it. It showed the opulent things she wanted. I couldn't imagine living like that. Simplicity for me was enough.

My favorite class was home economics. I could sew without a problem thanks to my mother and 4-H. I got done with my red polka dot circle skirt early and got to help the teacher make curtains for the sewing room. In knitting class, I made white mittens with a cable, but I made three stitches wrong. Everyone raved about the mittens anyway and wanted to put them in the school showcase. I said they could, but only if they put them so the three backwards stitches didn't show. I was not the best cook in cooking class but eager to learn. I learned to make a puffy omelet that fifty years later my husband wanted frequently for breakfast.

In junior high, for my birthday, Mother thought I needed to dress up like a young lady. That year, she got me lipstick and nylon stockings with the seam down the back and a garter belt to hold them up. Except for the fact that they were grown-up, it seemed to me they were a nuisance. Girls still wore skirts to school. Pants were not allowed. I preferred bobby socks to nylons and wore nylons only on Sunday.

If you figured that it was junior high when I started liking school, you would be right. We had a fancy semi-formal graduation. I needed a fancy dress to wear. I didn't have money to buy one. Dad made a deal with me. If I helped him haul logs for his new barn, he would pay for my graduation dress. He needed someone on the other end of the big bucksaw to balance it and help him roll the logs on to the wagon. He took them to the sawmill to be cut into boards. I wonder how many girls ever helped haul logs to get a fancy dress.

Mom took me shopping. We found a fluffy white strapless tea-length dress on sale. The dress had layers of nylon net on the skirt. I wasn't sure about the strapless part, but it did have a nylon net shawl that covered up most of what I didn't want to show. The graduation left me feeling like a princess in a dream. However, I couldn't understand why the committee had proclaimed my prophecy to be an explorer in South America. Well, I did like digging in the dirt. Anyway, what did they know? They weren't farmers.

Not too long after that, Dad started building the barn he had planned. The old one had to come down before it fell down. The new barn had a curved roof. Dad made a gig on the ground to shape the curve into the rafters. The siding was asbestos. Then no one knew it could cause cancer. The new barn served him well until he no longer was able to keep cows.

Dad believed that there is a God and believed the Bible. I remember one spring, he came in the house with a handful of dirt. Mom told him to take it outside, and he did. But not before he said, "There has got to be a God. Look at this dirt. There is nothing here, but put a seed in it and big plants grow. Who could have figured that out other than an all-knowing creator?"

7

In tenth grade, we got to go to the brand-new high school in Grand Haven. So much was new to me. It even had a swimming pool and a one-thousand-seat auditorium. Homerooms were new to me. Mine was 215 on the top floor. The library and study hall were on the other end of that floor. We reported to homeroom every morning for attendance and announcements. We kept our things in our very own locker with a combination lock. We only needed to remember the code to open it. The hallways had student monitors who kept the halls clear between classes. Girls were still required to wear skirts below their knees, and boys also had a dress code. If the monitors noticed anyone not dressed properly, they sent them to the office; likewise, if they were making trouble and not conforming to the rules, to the office they went.

The cafeteria and locker rooms for gym were on the basement level. We even had a rifle range, woodshop, and machine shop on that level. Also a recreation room where we could eat our lunch and hang out on our lunch break. Some of the kids played cards or table games. It was fun to watch a few kids dance to the new rock and roll music. I liked the hot lunches, so I mostly ate in the cafeteria.

Nursing school was my goal. As a result, my high school curriculum followed a college entry program. That required me to take a language. I decided Latin would be the most help in nursing. Well, it was a mistake. I don't think I ever got better than a D+. Beyond counting to ten in Latin, I can't recall anything I learned. I did like the teacher. She was very petite with delicate mannerisms and a sweet manner.

Geometry was a lot of homework, but I liked it. The teacher knew how to make it interesting. American history was dry; the teacher was retiring next year and recited everything in monotone from memory after her long years of doing it.

As a big shot of sixteen, my parents would allow me to date. My friend Nannette dated Roger, an eighteen-year-old guy who worked with her dad as a carpenter's helper. Roger usually brought his best buddy along on their dates. They went to football games or movies. Nanette convinced them to come the eight miles out in the country to pick me up so we could double date. That way, she didn't have to be alone with two boys. We double-dated that football season and went to a few movies. Roger's well-built but stocky buddy and I went to the movies a few times without them. I think we even held hands a couple times.

In February, my friend Nannette didn't want to go to the movie with her boyfriend Roger. He threatened to ask me, and she told him to do it. He called me and told me she said to ask me.

I didn't really want to go, so I tried to explain to my mother. "But Mom, he's Nannette's boyfriend."

"She told him to ask you. Go, it won't hurt anything."

I called Nannette to be sure. With her consent, I had my first date with tall, thin, dark blond, blue-eyed Roger to a movie on Valentine's Day. I didn't notice his buckteeth behind his big smile. But he was quick to tell me, "I am the only guy who could eat an ear of corn through a picket fence."

On the way to the movie, he gave me a card and a small heart box of candy. He said that he had planned it for Nanette, but since I was the one who was with him, it was mine. I didn't think I should keep it and felt a bit like I was second choice, but I was there and she wasn't. I think the movie was *The Creature from the Black Lagoon*. Can't say I enjoyed it. Monster movies were not my style.

That same night, Roger's friend, whom I had gone to the movies with a couple times, found out Roger and I had been to the movies. He actually was so mad that he tried cutting us off on the road on our way home. I was scared. But nothing happened. From then on, Roger was my steady date, and it wasn't long until he found a guy's class ring at a pawnshop, because he didn't have his own. I always wore it on a ribbon around my neck or on my finger with a big ball of tape as his steady girl. Thinking back, it saved me a lot of trouble. He had my class ring and wore it on his pinky.

Second semester in tenth grade, I took typing. The machine was foreign to me, and I had a seat by the window that faced the front of the school. I not only couldn't spell,

I was also distracted. The class ended during Roger's lunch break from work. He would drive by and pick me up after class so we could have lunch together. I watched for him out the window instead of paying attention to my typing. My parents even rented a typewriter for me to practice on, but I flunked typing class anyway.

I took home economics. Cooking was not my favorite. But sewing went well. By then, I had three years of 4-H sewing, three years of sewing in junior high, and would have two years in high school. I made a purple corduroy jumper with black triangles on it, also a pink printed sleeveless dress. The teacher asked me to help a classmate match plaid in the Bermuda shorts she was making. I felt proud to be able to help. I got an easy A in that class. Even though Latin and typing were not good, my other grades were.

I was blessed to take drivers training as a regular class and get a high school credit for it. One day, the instructor took three of us to the oval (now the City Park). He had me drive first because I had driven a tractor on the farm. Well, a tractor is different than a car. As we were going very slowly around a tight curve, instead of stepping on the brake to slow down, I stepped on the gas. We weren't going very fast, but it was just enough to get the front tire into the sand, and of course, we couldn't just back out. Lucky we had boys in the car who pushed, and we got out of the sand. Was I embarrassed!

Roger and I dated regularly and became a thing. We liked most of the same things, including anything out of doors and water-related. He lived with his mother and three brothers in a little house on the river.

March 11, my junior year, Roger went into the Army and did his two years. It was a blessing because he and I were getting way too serious. While he was gone, I was able to pay attention to schoolwork and got much better grades.

In summer, I continued to work in the fields for my dad and picked blueberries for a neighbor. Dad paid me twenty-five cents to hoe a long row. Getting up early, right after sunrise, allowed me to get more done before it got too hot. I got six cents a pound for picking blueberries. The most I ever picked was eighty pounds in a day. Probably, I would have earned more money working for my dad, but I wanted the social life that one got from the other kids at the berry patch and to be independent from my family. Besides, I hated picking beans and pickles in the hot sun. Blueberry bushes had a shady side.

As a junior, I was in library club at school. That meant we took our turn helping out in the library. I learned the Dewey decimal system, how to properly open a new book, how to check out books, and what cleanser was best to clean the sink. My mom thought I was serious when I told her how white Comet made the sink. We used it in the library. Mother started using it at home too.

I was required to take physical education one year. I could still not keep up in sports, but I could swim like a fish. I wanted to join the swimming club, but it was after school and I didn't have a ride home. I did manage to get on the prom committee where the juniors put on the prom for the seniors. By then, I could drive and borrow my parents' car. The school had always used the country club in Spring Lake for prom in the past. But it was not available. We had a problem. When we started to consider other options, we realized that we had a brand-new gym that we could convert. Some thought it wouldn't be good enough, but we put our heads together and nearly covered the ceiling with balloons. Sand was hauled in to make islands of sand with palm trees. The theme was Bali Hai, with island music of course. Everyone seemed amazed at the atmosphere that we created. I needed a dress because juniors could go to the prom too. But Roger was in Germany, and my dad didn't want to go with me. I still needed a dress because I helped out on the food committee. I bet I was the only girl who helped her dad haul logs to earn her prom dress. Yup, I wore the same dress I wore for ninth-grade graduation. But I added a bunch of little lavender bows all over so it didn't seem the same to me.

Dad encouraged my sister and I to raise strawberries and sell them for profit. He loaned us a couple acres and worked up the ground for us. We put our heart and soul into planting them, hoeing them, picking them, and taking them to market. I made enough to buy half of my parents' old car, a '47, green, two-door Chevy. They gave me the other half for my birthday. I drove it to school in my senior year because I was a nurse aide student (Bluebird) and helped at the local hospital after school. So I was not able to take the bus home. Raising strawberries was a great experience. I learned to plan and be responsible from this experience.

Thankfully, I had drivers training, but there are things you don't learn in class and driving with an instructor. Like if you park on ice, the warm tires sink in, and you will spin all day and just make it worse. I stopped at the store, and that's what happened. Some nice guy gave me a push. I had more respect for ice after that. Then there was the cold snowy day the car broke down on the way to town. We didn't have cell phones then, so I had to walk to the nearest house, at least a block, just to call for help. I was cold, and it took a long time for someone to come to the door. The lady wasn't sure she trusted me, but she left me outside and made the call for me. For the most part, I was proud of that car. Mostly kids with rich dads had cars, not the average high school senior.

That year, I didn't go to football games except for once. Friends asked me to go with them to the game, so I did, but I was not alone in the back seat. We picked up her brother along the way. Instead of football, we went somewhere else. I just remember the guy tried to put his arm around me, and I felt like they had conspired to set me up with this guy. I let them know in no uncertain terms that I was Roger's girl and not interested.

I wrote to Roger every day. If I couldn't think of anything, I simply wrote I love you. It was affordable as stamps were only three cents each then. If he was in the field on maneuvers, he could not write to me for a couple weeks, so of course, I worried. Once if I had known I would have been in a real mess. Later he told me he had had a flu or something and had a very high fever with something like one hundred seven temperature. He said he had weird dreams during the fever. If I remember correctly, he said they had mats on the floor of the gym because so many were sick. I don't know if anyone died from it. I was just happy that Roger was okay.

He never saw combat. They were peacekeepers, and they went on maneuvers to keep in shape. He was very good with an M-1 rifle and became a sharpshooter. He was so good that after the Army, he decided not to be a hunter because he figured he had an unfair advantage.

At school, my homeroom teacher was the speech teacher and also directed school plays. Once I tried out for a play but could barely get the words out for fear. However, when assignments came out, the director had assigned me to be the head of the house committee. We were the ones who did the ushering and greeting people. He assigned a few other girls, but I was in charge. I was a senior then and had a car, so I was able to work the play around my nurse aide time. We had to dress formal. I took the dress I used for the prom the year before and adapted it again. This time, I used the shawl to make a gathered boa to go around my shoulders and attached it to the dress so it looked like an off-the-shoulder collar.

Nurse aide class was what I had wanted more than anything so I could get a head start on being a nurse. The class would qualify me to be a CNA (certified nurse aide in today's language). We had the cutest blue-green jumpers and white blouses. We had to wear white shoes and stockings. That was in the day when nurses wore white uniforms. I got to watch a baby being born and got to help feed babies in the nursery. I loved working with children in the hospital. One of my favorite kids was Chuck Rose who had his appendix out. He was only four years younger than me. His appendix had burst, so he had to stay extra-long to heal and be sure he didn't get an infection. Working on the surgical floor was rewarding. People usually got better and went home. It was not so fun taking care of grumpy old people on the medical floor, but one old geezer invited me in bed with him. I was shocked, but now I laugh about it.

About then, the home economics teacher and the nurse aide teacher told me they thought I should go into home economics rather that nursing. I wasn't sure that was a good idea. My mom said that she didn't think there were many jobs for home economics majors, but there were always jobs for nurses. Besides, she always wanted to be a nurse, but her dad wouldn't let her. He didn't think it a proper profession for a woman. So Mother thought I should go into nursing so I wouldn't have regrets. My mom said that the only things a woman could do in those days was be a secretary or a teacher. I had really wanted to be a doctor, but she convinced me that women weren't doctors. So I settled for nursing. Looking back, I think I may have been better at home economies than nursing.

When the LPN association offered me a scholarship for practical nurse training in Grand Rapids to cover my tuition and books, Mom convinced me to take it. I still had to come up with room and board. Mother was happy. I also had a chance to train for psychiatric nursing for free with room and board included, but Mom thought it was too far away, and she didn't think she wanted me to work with the mentally ill.

What to do for room and board? We could spend a lot of money for a room, or I could live with someone and help with housework. So we went to Grand Rapids and interviewed for a nanny position, also for a part-time maid. The nanny position sounded good to me, but Mother thought that wouldn't leave me much time for homework. Besides, they had a boy about my age, and she didn't like that idea. So I settled for the maid position. It was an older couple with no children.

High school graduation was amazing. It was held in the auditorium. Two hundred and twelve seniors lined up outside on a beautiful spring day. All of us walked together into the auditorium and sat in the front rows. The remainder of seats were occupied by family and friends. I still remember how surprised I was when my aunt from Clarksville stopped over with a gift a few days later. The gift was a bracelet with a clear glass bubble on it. Inside the bubble was a grain of mustard seed. A verse was in the box. It said, "If you have the faith of a grain of mustard seed nothing shall be impossible to you." It was from the Bible. It has been a hope and courage for me throughout my whole life.

Summer was fun. I had a job at the Dairy Queen on Water Street. I got really good at making the curl on top of the cone. Who wouldn't like to eat all the ice cream you wanted and have boys flirting with you? I could have dated, but I was Roger's girl and wore that ring around my neck to prove it. That summer, I learned what a Pronto Pup was. They were right across the street.

In the fall, I moved to Grand Rapids and started school.

PART 2

Real life

8

While in Grand Rapids, I stayed with an older childless couple. She had arthritis and much pain. A rather cute little old lady type yet she still stood straight and put on her makeup every day. Was her hair gray or was it blond? Either way, it was light. She was always neatly dressed. I remember hearing her on the phone. People would ask her how she was. Her response invariably would be "Terrible." She then would go on to relate every ache and pain, real or imagined. That was hard for me because I came from a home where we didn't talk much about our aches and pains but just kept tugging forward.

Her husband was short, thin, nervous, yet patient. Always immaculately dressed, his dark hair and dark eyes make him the perfect executive type. He worked at an office job and rode the bus to work. Their shiny classic car stayed in the garage except on very special occasions.

They provided me with a nice room and uniforms so I looked the part of the maid. Big deal, I didn't know much about being a maid. I helped prepare meals, set the table, and served them in their formal dining room. I ate in the maid's room next to the dining room. If they wanted anything, she used her foot to push a button on the floor under the table that rang the bell for me to come and wait on them. They also had a housekeeper come in and do the main housework. I had to help cook, set the table, do dishes, light housework, and keep up my own room. She tried to have me do laundry, but apparently, I didn't do it right. After a couple tries, she hired it out. I remember they had a carpet sweeper for me to use on the floor. Sometimes I had to do it over again because I missed a couple specks of dust on the carpet.

My mother was an excellent housekeeper, but this seemed extreme to me. I missed the things at home, especially my little brothers and sisters, the animals, and the open space. I even missed the sewing machine. However, I did manage to sew myself a pair of wool-lined pants with a zipper all by hand. I wore them often. They fit just right and held up very well.

I wrote to Roger every day and did my homework. I did above average schoolwork but not up to what I did in high school. Once, the nursing director called me into her office and wanted to know why I wasn't doing better. She said that tests showed I was capable of more. Perhaps I was homesick. I can't say that I was really happy there. I liked the walk to the bus stop every day and then a maybe twenty-minute bus ride so I could look at the city. That just served to make me miss the country more. Buildings were crammed in next to each other and left little room for trees.

School was right where the old campus is to today, Grand Rapids Junior (community) College. The first day there, we had orientation. One of the girls told our group, "If you don't smoke, you are out of the crowd." Well, that did it. I was not going to inhale that horrible smelling smoke. I would just be out of it. Transportation and work kept me from getting involved in extracurricular activities. I didn't get to go home on weekends much, but I enjoyed walking. On occasion, I went to a movie. The theater was close enough that I could walk. My favorite was Pat Boone in *State Fair*. I even walked the several blocks home alone in the dark. No one bothered me or thought anything of it. One Sunday, a girl that rode the same bus as me and I went for a walk. We walked and walked and got a bit lost. We found where they were building the bypass. Using our sense of direction on a sunny day, we found our way back.

My first time at a hospital for training was so scary. It was at Blodgett and so big compared to North Ottawa at that time. I don't think I remember any of it except how scared I was. Near the end of the semester, I was called into the office again. I thought the director would tell me I couldn't continue. Instead, she asked if I would like to move home and complete my training at Holland Hospital.

Inside, I felt like I wanted to jump up and down. That was great for me. I still had my car. I could live at home and drive back and forth. Missing the family and not feeling comfortable at the big hospital, I could hardly wait. Five or six of us would train there. We would still have to go to Grand Rapids for some classes, but most of the time, we would have our classes at Holland. Our instructor had to drive from Grand Rapids. She had the cutest car. It was a three-wheeled Isetta. Not sure how it was spelled. The front opened up instead of regular doors. I wanted a car like that.

I liked Holland Hospital better. My favorite place was pediatrics. There were a couple children who had bad burns. I got to give them a bath every day and played games with them. Sometimes I got to be in charge on the pediatrics unit because it was so small. The RN on the medical floor next door was my backup. Usually, there were only two or three pediatrics patients at one time.

Having my own car was good, and I remember paying twenty-five cents a gallon for gas. The attendant came out to the car and pumped the gas, checked the oil, and washed the windows. It's no wonder that I long for the good old days.

They were building the new US-31 four-lane divided highway at that time. It wasn't finished, so I took a two-lane road. I think it was old US-31 or 136th Avenue. It came out at River Road in Holland. The hospital was south of Holland where it is today, but the driving was easy.

One day, it had snowed hard during the day. On my way home, I got within a quarter mile of home on our seldom-traveled gravel road. The snow was so deep, I had

THE LIFE OF A SPOILED BRAT

trouble getting through. It pulled me into the ditch, and I of course couldn't move the car. So I had to walk the rest of the way home with no boots. My dad took the tractor and pulled the car out.

That Christmas, Roger sent me a gift from Germany. In it was a satin pillow cover with a verse on it. It really said a lot to me. It said:

> Sweetheart, I thought that you would like to know
> That someone's thoughts go where you go.
> That someone never can forget
> The hours we spent since we first met.
> That life is richer sweeter far
> For such a sweetheart as you are
> And now my constant prayer will be
> That God will keep you safe for me.

I don't remember the author.

9

In March, Roger came home before I expected. He called me from the Muskegon Airport to pick him up. I was supposed to go to the hospital and take a test for school that day. I tried to beg out of picking him up. He said that he thought he would surprise me and didn't understand why school was more important than seeing him. Besides, he didn't have anyone else to come for him. I picked him up having a guilt trip for skipping school but happy to see him home safe.

In a couple days, we were sitting on my parents' living room couch holding hands. He leaned over and quietly told me, "We are engaged. I will be getting you a ring as soon as I get discharged."

I think I simply said, "Okay." Then we kissed.

Sure enough, when he got his discharge in Illinois, he came home with a very pretty ring set with a nice small diamond and tiny diamonds on each side. The wedding ring matched.

I would graduate in September, but we were in a hurry to be married, so we had a July wedding. I was still going to

Holland for training. We got an upstairs furnished apartment on Pennoyer Street in Grand Haven. The front inside stairs stopped at a hall that had the bathroom, the bedroom, and living room doors. The back stairs were outside and came into the small kitchen. We parked in back and used the back stairs. The laundry, with a wringer washer, was in the basement. We hung the clothes on the line outside.

Roger's mother used his car while he was gone. When he got back, she got her own car. She was working as a housekeeper at the local hospital. He got his car back so he and I both had transportation. He had a job second shift at Oldbergs, a muffler factory on the north side of town. He got about three dollars an hour. It was good wages then. I got fifty cents an hour for helping at Holland Hospital as a student. We thought we were okay.

Our wedding was nice. We were married at the Lutheran Church that we had joined together. He had been catholic and I evangelical and reformed. Because we each had a grandparent who was Lutheran, we figured that was a good compromise. The only problem, because the wedding was not in the Catholic Church, Roger's best friend could not be in it. Roger's other best friend couldn't because he was away in the Army. So for his attendants, Roger had his brother Joe and other best friend's brother Tyrone.

I made my long white satin dress with a huge bow on the back and long pointed sleeves. Mother picked out the pattern and the fabric. Good thing too, because I would have picked out something lacy and ruffly. I had a hard enough time sewing the simple lines of the pattern she picked. I cried when I made a mistake and just knew the place where I had to take out stitches stood out like a sore thumb.

My sister Judy, my cousin Bonnie, and friend Marilyn were my attendants. My sister, my mom, and Grandmother made the tea-length dresses, one medium green, one yellow, and one pink taffeta. All from the same pattern as my dress minus the bow. The guys wore their dress suits. Tux rental seemed like throwing money away.

The wedding went well. I don't remember most of it. I just remember my dad almost ran me down the aisle like he was in a hurry to be rid of me. Probably he just wanted the wedding over. From then on, it was a blur.

The reception was at the township hall. My mom and some other volunteers spent much of the day putting the food together. Mom even made the three-tiered wedding cake. Most people knew that Mom was a wonderful cook. As usual, the food was great. My aunt provided the flowers from her garden. The daisies were beautiful. My cousin took pictures. He was an amateur photographer and developed his own pictures. Somewhere in the process, most of them were lost. A few negatives were saved. Even so, pictures don't make a marriage.

We did have beer for the beer drinkers and dancing. Dad had to have a bit of a German wedding. Late in the evening, there was a fight outside, and police were called. It must not have been too bad because I never heard more about it. When it was time to leave, Roger and I found our car covered with crepe paper streamers and a "Just Married" sign on the back.

For our honeymoon, Roger chose to surprise me by taking me across the river to a motel. The next morning, he planned to buy us breakfast, but nothing was open on Sunday morning in those days. We had bought groceries and put them in our new apartment a couple days before. So we ended up at our apartment only to find broken eggs wrapped in paper towel in a pan on the stove and Jell-O water in the bathtub. I was shocked, and Roger was not happy. Lucky for us, the bedroom had a separate door with a keylock. We had the key. I am sure we would have found trouble in there too. Later in the morning, my parents brought the gifts over for us. We enjoyed each other and the gifts. We stayed at the apartment because I had to go to school the next day.

Roger was working second shift at his factory job. A couple months later, the union decided to strike, and we were out of that paycheck. The fifty cents an hour that I got would end when I graduated. *No problem, nursing jobs would be easy to get,* I thought.

10

I finished school and graduated in September. It was so sad because my mom couldn't go to my graduation. My brothers were sick. By then, I knew I was pregnant but didn't show under that white uniform. We got a white cap with a gray stripe, so we felt proud of being a nurse. I immediately went to our local hospital to get the job I had been promised, but they didn't have work. As I look back, there was a depression. They did use me occasionally on call, but we had no phone so the nursing director would come over and see if I could work.

I had been having morning sickness all day every day. Cooking meat was near impossible without throwing up. The hospital mostly used me on the night shift. Nausea didn't seem to be as much of a problem at night. No matter, I didn't work much anyway. Without a steady paycheck, we couldn't make the rent payments, so we were asked to move.

Roger was promised a job with the builder that he worked for as a carpenter's helper in the past. They had started a basement house that someone wanted then backed out on. The builder let us move into it after some improvements were made. We did have thirty days to move from the apartment so there was time to get the basement ready. We celebrated our first Christmas in that basement. We even had a Christmas tree. The builders would help Roger build the house on top and finance it too. We painted basement walls and floor, put up a divider wall for a bedroom and another for the toilet. As I recall, the septic was already in. But we had to elevate the toilet and had a pump to pump up the waste.

I never did work much, but Roger worked when the builders had work. That was very little in winter. By then, he could get some unemployment because when the strike ended, the shopworkers were laid off. The shop still paid our insurance.

By then, we knew for sure I was pregnant and was gaining some weight. Mother got me a couple sack dresses and decided I needed a coat. She took Roger and me shopping to Sears in Holland. I found a coat I really liked. She thought I should have a different one. Roger agreed with her. I was not happy, but she was buying. We got the one she wanted. It was a good coat, full enough to cover a pregnant tummy. Still it was a reminder that Mother usually told me what to get anyway. Is it any wonder I am not a shopper today and don't like to make decisions? Mother was good at helping me decide.

In May, Susan was born. I spent many hours carrying her around. Even operating the wringer washer with her in one arm. I loved it when I was folding clothes while sitting on the couch with her sitting in the corner. She would talk to me in her sweet baby talk. It wasn't long until one of her favorite games was dropping things out of the highchair for us to pick up.

When spring came, work began on the top of the house. It turned out to be a very nice three-bedroom ranch. I had a pink countertop stove and pink built-in oven. I think a pink sink too. The bathroom had blue fixtures. I was still a bit spoiled. The bedrooms and living room had bare wood floors. Carpet would come later.

One nice summer day, while we were there, I decided to surprise my mom who lived only about two miles away on gravel roads. We didn't have a phone, so I couldn't call to warn her. I put Susan in the old baby buggy and headed down the road walking. It was hard pushing the buggy, but we made it. I was wiped out when we got there. It turns out Mom was in the middle of something. She told me, "I'm sorry, but I'm busy." That made sense because she had a preschooler and two elementary boys to keep up with and still tried to help Dad. My sister Betty tried to help Mom in the house, and Judy helped Dad in the fields. I turned around and cried most of the way home. It brought back memories of when I was young and wanted to talk. So often I would hear, "Don't bother me, I'm busy." After that, I tried not to bother anyone without an invitation. Lucky for me, Roger was a little bolder, or I would have become a hermit way back then. He was good at picking up and visiting people.

Sometime about then, I remembered that it said in the Bible, "All things work together for good." It was an encouragement to me. I didn't know where in the Bible it was or what the rest of it said. Even so, I clung to it and the verse from the bracelet. If you have the faith of a grain of mustard seed, nothing shall be impossible to you. I was not a Bible reader and did not memorize verses. But somehow I knew there is a God and he is good.

11

Roger's factory first had a strike then laid off most everyone. I think the company lost so much business during the strike and recession that they didn't have work. Thankfully, the health insurance was still good, because I got pregnant again. We still lived in the basement.

I always wanted a big family. My grandma had twins. I thought that was wonderful, so I prayed hard for twins. God answered my prayers. I knew I was carrying twins, but the doctor thought he could only hear one heartbeat. He thought he heard an echo but not a second heart. They didn't do ultrasounds then. However, I was gaining weight too fast. So he gave me pills to reduce the fluid. I took only one or two and stopped because they made me feel strange. Later those pills were taken off the market. I don't know why. I could feel a strong kick and a flutter. But even in the delivery room, after a hard delivery, Jean was born. The doctor was looking at Jean's large umbilical hernia. When the nurse said, as she was massaging my abdomen to contract the uterus and reduce the excessive bleeding, "Doctor, there is another baby in here." By then, I was bleeding excessively from a difficult delivery. So they made haste to hurry the delivery of Joan. Joan was perfectly formed but small, only four and a half pounds compared to Jean's seven something. I had twins! My prayers were answered.

Jean had surgery on the first day for the umbilical hernia, and they kept her in a separate isolation nursery. Joan was in an incubator. She was tiny and had to have drops to keep her food down. I was not in good shape as they almost lost me in the delivery due to excessive bleeding. I remember massaging my own tummy so it would stay firm so I wouldn't bleed so much. I went home after a week with no babies and very weak. I had never even gotten to hold my babies.

Jean had surgery when she was one day old and was never healthy. Joan came home after about three weeks. They let us bring Jean home about a week later. I will never forget, when Susan saw Jean, she went back and forth between the two cribs saying, "Two babies, two babies." Jean was five weeks when she died from a bowel obstruction.

Not being well myself, taking care of sick babies and a two-year-old was all I could do, but I loved it. We only had Jean home for about one week before she had to go back to the hospital. I am so thankful for that week, even though I got very little sleep. It still pains me to think about watching Jean die because there was nothing they could do. I remember watching as tan liquid came out of her nose and mouth and her taking her last breaths. She was buried in a sweet baby blue dress and had a little casket with white and, I think, tiny rosebuds on the lining. Her tiny body is buried in Babyland in the Grand Haven cemetery.

For a year after that, I wasn't right; maybe I never was. Anyway, Sue was a helper by then. Once, I had Joan on the floor in the living room to let her stretch and an easy place for a diaper change. After I took off her diaper, I went to get a washcloth. When I got back, Sue had powdered the floor and Joan, trying to "Help Mom."

We needed the money, but work was scarce. I tried going back to work but was weak. The first day, Roger was supposed to babysit. What did he do? He took the girls to a friend of his and left them with the wife while the guys went to play at something. Fishing, I think. I did not even know the people at all; I had never met them. That did it. I would take care of my own kids.

We were so poor that one day, we got up and did not have anything but pancakes for breakfast and a little milk for the girls. There would be no money for a day or two until Roger got his unemployment check. The mail came at ten in the morning. In it was a ten-dollar check from someone who had owed Roger from way back. It was enough to get us through. It reminded me that God sees our needs and takes care of those who love and believe in him.

Even so, we couldn't make the eighty-dollars-a-month house payment. Someone suggested we sell the house and move into my grandma's little one-bedroom house; it was empty. She was living in an assisted living home by then. So we put our pretty house up for sale. Someone from Muskegon fell in love with my dream house. We let it go in exchange for a small cash down payment and their two-apartment house in Muskegon. We could rent it to help us out, or we could live in it and the other apartment could pay the rent. One apartment in the Muskegon house was already rented. As I type this, I feel like crying.

12

We moved into Grandma's little house across the field from my parents and liked it. Roger still did not have regular work, but he rented farmland nearby and worked his heart out preparing the soil, planting, and cultivating. He even bought a tractor on credit to make it work. He rented another piece of land to grow lettuce. The garden was doing very well. We were eating some of the produce. Then a neighbor's cows got out of their fence and devoured our beautiful crop. They ate watermelons, tomatoes, cucumbers, and I don't remember what else. There was nothing left to take to market. At least we still had the lettuce crop. It was about perfect and ready to harvest. Roger went there one day, and the whole field had been reduced to stubble. A herd of deer had come through and flattened the whole field. I hoped they had tummy aches.

That same fall, I was coming home from town. The two girls were with me. Sue was standing on the front seat, and Joan was lying next to her. Child seats were not heard of then. Joan started crying. Sue tried to give her the bottle but was not successful. So I looked down to do it. When I looked up, a large tree was directly in front of me. Thankfully, I was only going about thirty miles per hour. My left arm broke as it hit the steering wheel. Susan and Joan landed on the floor in front. I think I knocked them down with my right arm so they wouldn't hit the windshield. Thankfully, it happened in front of a farmer's house. He came out and called for help. We had an ambulance ride to the emergency room. The girls were okay, but now I would spend the next six weeks with my arm in a cast, trying to take care of two little ones and keep a discouraged husband happy. It seems he was not destined to be a farmer, but I think he may have enjoyed it. The apartment in Muskegon had not rented, and we decided to move there. Grandma's house would be sold.

Living in an upstairs apartment in mid-winter in Muskegon proved to be interesting. One of the three bedrooms was nothing but an unfinished attic under the slanted roof. The other was a tiny room the size of a small bathroom or walk-in closet. The main bedroom was barely sufficient. But it would do. The living room and kitchen were fine. We had Christmas there. Roger's family came, and we had a good time. I remember Roger's brother Joe got down on the floor with Susan, and he let her butt heads with him. By then, I was about five months pregnant, and Joan was still so tiny.

One night, the downstairs renter yelled up the stairs that someone was stealing our car. It was parked in the backyard. Being trusting people, we had left the keys in the car. It was a cold snowy night with drifting snow. The police were called. The joke was on the robber. The car got stuck in a snowdrift before it even got out of the alley to the street. The police followed the foot tracks but had no luck finding the guy. Needless to say, keys were not left in the car after that.

It was obvious I couldn't work. There were no LPN jobs anyway; besides, I was pregnant. There had been ads for over-the-road truck drivers. Roger found an ad where they would train if you signed on for a certain length of time. In the meantime, at seven months, my water broke, and the doctor said, "Bed rest." So when Roger went to Indiana for truck driving training, my parents took me and the kids in. A couple weeks into the training, my contractions started. My mom was at work, so my dad drove me and the kids to the hospital and dropped me off. He took the kids back with him. I was there by myself and scared as I could be, afraid the baby would die. It was two months early, and we lost a baby a year before. I prayed that the baby would be healthy and not die. All I wanted was a healthy baby. Knowing this one was early made it all the worse. My parents tried to get ahold of Roger. Finally, after a few hours, they did. By the time he got back home, Nancy was born three and one-half healthy pounds. She was little but perfect.

Roger was so angry because he wasn't there that he took it out on my mom verbally. He blamed her for not letting him know sooner. Forgetting she was at work and that they had tried but couldn't get through. When I left the hospital, Roger had moved us into a big drafty farmhouse closer to home. Nancy was a good eater and gained weight fast.

THE LIFE OF A SPOILED BRAT

We were able to bring her home soon. Thankfully, the shop insurance was still good.

Another new adventure. The farmhouse was huge compared to the little apartment. It had three upstairs bedrooms and a downstairs bedroom, a very large living room, dining room, and kitchen. Not many cupboards. Plus an adequate bathroom. I liked it. The main drawback was it was cold and drafty. Impossible to keep heated. That winter, we had the girls sleeping downstairs in the dining area where it was warmer.

When Nancy was a few months old, she had a cold that came on pretty fast. One night, she could barely breathe. I called the doctor. He told me to bring her in in the morning. Knowing what I know now, I would have taken her to the emergency right then. That night, I sat with her in the rocking chair and held her to me, rocking to be sure she kept breathing. I took her to the doctor in the morning. She was looking blue and gasping for breath. By then, she had a bad case of pneumonia. He told me to take her to the emergency in our little local hospital. They immediately put her on 100 percent oxygen and gave her antibiotics. It didn't help. *Maybe it kept her alive.* They told us there was a new antibiotic, but it hadn't been fully tested. They would like to try it on her. We said okay. So they tried it. It worked. But the drug was taken off the market later because of side effects. I had been in a panic as I couldn't stand to lose another baby. The relief of being able to take her home was so great. As she got older, her teeth came in discolored from that drug, but she was alive.

Things seemed to be settling down. The little ones and I were adjusting. Roger found a job as a car salesman on commission and the use of a brand-new car. He was good at it. One had to sell a car to make any money. He started doing good; we were surviving but still behind on the rent. So the landlord told Roger we had to move again. Roger was angrier than I had ever seen him. He wrote profanities on the inside of the back porch. Thankfully, he didn't wreck anything.

This time, we rented a house in town, a sweet little two-bedroom house. I went to work. All they had was night shift, and Roger was working at the car lot. I had to sleep sometime. I slept while Roger was home in the evening and while the kids took a nap. One day, I woke up to Susan standing on the toilet getting baby aspirin out for the kids, trying to help. If I remember correctly, I had to make one of them throw up because they had had some, and we didn't know how much. Another time, I got up to Susan sticking a table knife into the toaster to get toast out to feed the kids. She was my helper at five years old, always trying to help. In desperation, I started bringing the kids into the bedroom while I slept and blocking the door. It wasn't working. Roger was doing okay, so I quit the job.

In an effort to help make some money, I took in sewing and set up a sewing area in the basement. Roger was doing quite well at the car sales. And we enjoyed the use of the new cars. Finally, things started turning around.

Oh yes, another adventure while we were there; the next-door neighbor came over early one morning and wanted to use our phone. She said she had just given birth and had her baby at home. She had a couple other very young boys and her husband was in jail. She needed to use the phone. She actually made her own call to the ambulance. I was barely awake and either low blood pressure from getting up too fast or low sugar, I nearly passed out. I sat on the floor, then somehow, I got it together and went over to see what I could do. I checked the baby. It was okay. She had not cut the cord, and I knew it was okay to leave it for a short time since the ambulance was on the way. They came and handled things.

13

By then, Nancy was almost two, Joan three, and Susan was five. In May, she would have to start school. Roger and I had had it and decided we needed a new start. Maybe we were running away. We searched until Roger found a car sales job in Klamath Falls, Oregon. He could start as soon as we got there. So Roger built a box for the top of the Pontiac we had gotten from my dad and packed up what we could, then sold or gave away the rest. We took the back seat out of the car and put in the cedar chest filled with clothes and whatever we thought we needed. Seatbelts were unheard of and no baby seat was required. We made a comfortable bed on top of the cedar chest and other things. The girls seemed to like it, but to this day, Susan said it was not comfortable. They didn't complain. We packed the box on top of the car with as much of our stuff as we could. We had enough money to get us there and rent someplace to stay and had planned a couple stops to sleep on the way.

We had a going away get-together at Roger's mother's the day before, and in the morning, we left early and we stopped at my parents. The kids still remember the box of Lucky Charms Grandma gave them. They traveled well and seldom complained. They could take naps on the platform we had fixed, and we had snacks for them. I was worried that the car might not make it. I prayed for God to help us. I saw in my mind the hand of God reaching down and holding the engine together. We made it to Iowa the first day. Got a motel and started out again early the next morning.

The only mishap we had was when Roger misjudged the height of the box on top of the car and drove under a drive-up restaurant canopy. Oops, that shifted the load, so it had to be unloaded and repacked, taking up precious time. We traveled until dark and found a motel in Wyoming somewhere. They had a restaurant attached. We ordered chili. We had never had western chili. Neither Roger nor I could eat; it was so hot. So how could the kids? The restaurant people gave us something else, but I don't remember what. The next day was a memorable drive. I remember that there were not many towns, and the population seemed rather sparse. We had driven on two-lane highways most of the way. We saw even more scenery, large lava flows in Idaho and desert, salt flats in Utah, or was that another trip?

When we got to Oregon, we thought we were almost there. So we drove over mountains and high desert and drove and drove until finally we got there. We came over a hill late in the afternoon. There it was! We needed a place to stay. We needed to conserve our money, and the town had very little to rent, but we asked and found a motel that was being used for transient rentals, very reasonable. We stayed there in the two bedrooms. The girls slept three crosswise in the bed. It was clean and had a kitchen and bathroom. That was all we needed. There was a railroad track almost up against the back of the motel and a wringer washer in the laundry in a garage at the back, just in front of the tracks. The train was slow and noisy. I didn't let the girls outside unless I was with them. Roger was able to start work right away. We would live there for six weeks.

14

We found Zion Lutheran Church Missouri Synod to attend the first Sunday. That was the denomination we had attended in Grand Haven. They basically adopted us. Life in Oregon seemed like it would be a great adventure. We indeed had a place to start over.

Not only did the church people adopt us, the first Sunday they invited us to a potluck that same day, and we didn't have to bring anything. One of the members invited me and the three little ones to a Bible study that very week, and she even picked us up. We could pack her two and my three all in the back seat. I enjoyed the Wednesday morning Bible study every week. We all brought our own kids. The girls enjoyed playing with the other kids. Kids there seemed very respectful and did as they were told most of the time.

The best lesson I learned at the Bible study was when one of the members told us that Jesus is a gift to us, like if someone gives us a gift. If we set it aside or reject it, it's not ours. But if we open it and accept it, it's ours. I envisioned getting a gift and setting it aside and not opening it. I wouldn't know what I was missing. If I opened it, that was the most precious thing I had ever received.

The only drawback at Bible study was I learned to drink coffee. I felt uneasy being the only one who drank just water and didn't want them to go to the trouble of making me tea. When they saw that I only had water, they would fuss until I let them make me tea or something special, so I started drinking coffee with milk and sugar. Gradually, I learned to drink it black. I have been drinking it that way ever since.

One nice summer day at Bible study, the kids were playing outdoors and got into a hill of fire ants. They all had fiery bites and a red rash. That ended the study for the day.

After a few weeks, I was really shocked when they asked me to lead the lesson. I learned we all took turns. That included me. We used old junior high Sunday school curriculum and basically just went around and gave people turns to answer the questions in the book. In the fall, they had a training for Sunday school teachers. I took it and, after a time, started teaching kindergarten, or preschool.

The public schools there had no kindergarten. But we wanted Sue to go in case we went back to Michigan; she would not be behind. We were able to find a church that had kindergarten. So we paid the low tuition to Bible Baptist Kindergarten. Sue did well, as did Joan two years later.

Six weeks after we got to Klamath Falls, we found a sweet house with three bedrooms, a fireplace, and a narrow kitchen. The breeze way had been made into an extra room. You had to go through it to get to the garage. The house itself was lower than the road on a slight hill. Drainage was no problem due to the forethought of someone in the past. Along the road, we had a carport with three stalls. Maybe it was from the old horse and buggy days. The house was partly furnished and had a washer and dryer. A friend from church provided us with the furniture we still needed from the backroom of his loan company. Apple trees grew in the backyard, and we had a nice garden plot that we hoped to use.

The neighbors across the street were Native American. I loved hearing the stories from the grandmother. She talked about how at one time they lived in a cave. One morning, she woke up with a snake inside her nightgown. I would have loved to sit and listen to her all day. They seemed always to be busy canning, drying, and preserving for the future. Three generations lived there. The youngest was just around my girl's age. He would come and play with the girls sometimes.

I was busy with three kids and was pregnant for a fourth. Across the field was a neighbor with a teenaged girl. She was a good babysitter that the girls liked.

We made friends, mostly from church. The Herts and the Johnsons were almost instant friends. We were invited to their place for a meal or a picnic, and we had them to our place.

To this day, I can't help wondering if that Thanksgiving we entertained a future president unawares. We had invited Elna and Jimmy Johnson and their two boys over for dinner. They asked if they could bring their guests from out of town. Of course, we would be happy to have them. They brought Bill and Nancy Johnson. He was very tall and well-built. Reminded me of Ronald Reagan in the movies. She was petite with dark hair. They clung to each other like newlyweds. She sat on his lap for much of the afternoon.

At dinner, we talked about his experiences in the movies and working for Tennessee Ernie Ford on his ranch. He said that he had been a stand-in and stuntman in some movies and told us stories about living in the Wild West. At one point after dinner, he asked how we felt about the candidate for president, Ronald Reagan. Having a big mouth and being judgmental, I blurted out something like, "I think that he could be a great president, but I don't like that he married the divorcée Nancy." It seemed like he was ready to leave right there, but Nancy calmed him down and convinced him to stay. After that, the conversation was limited.

They remained in town for a few weeks and came to church on Sunday. I noticed that he always wore an expensive-looking leather belt with hand-carving on it. It clearly said Johnson across the back. He always wore cowboy boots and western-style clothing, including a big western hat. They didn't stop to talk much, just slipped in and out. At some time, I asked my friend Elna about his name, but she acted like she didn't know what I was talking about. End of story, but I will always wonder.

That first Christmas looked like it would be pretty sparse. We did manage to get a permit to go into the forest and cut our own Christmas tree. We had brought a few decorations from Michigan, and we had fun making a few more, like paper bells, chains, and popcorn chains. The tree looked nice, but we had little to put under it. Surprise, in the mail came a box from my parents containing a gift for each of us. Then Roger came home with gifts for the kids from fellow employees. Someone gave us the cutest little black puppy. We neither had nor thought about a kennel for it. A box with a cushion would do. Christmas morning, we got up to gifts all over the living room with scraps of wrapping paper everywhere. The puppy had opened most of the presents, puppy style. I still can see red yarn strewn all around. It was a gift from my mother for me to knit something. I was able to salvage most of it to use later. I don't think anything was ruined, but it sure was a shock.

Roger must have mentioned at work that I could make anything grow because one day, he came home with a large nearly dead plant. He said that someone at work had given it to him and said, "Take this home and see if your wife can do something with it, or else we have to throw it away." It was easy to revive. I pruned it back to a few green leaves. Soon it was lush, green, and growing rapidly.

At that house, I learned about canal irrigation. Several canals ran from Klamath Lake through the town. In the dry season, people could open the gates that let the water run into small ditches beside the roads. When gardeners needed water, they could open the gates to their garden and let the water run into their garden. It worked well since most of the ground was not totally level. Someone must have planned it so that they could take advantage of the hills.

I also I learned about earwigs. What's that? It's a fairly active, wiggly bug, about maybe one inch long. The apple trees in the yard had ripe apples on it, so I picked one and cut it open. Out popped a couple, wiggling, fast-moving bugs. I had never seen them before and was horrified. I dropped the apple and didn't try anymore. I don't think they bite, but I wasn't about to find out. I learned they love fruit and will hide in cracks of trees or anywhere there was a crack.

Susan rode the bus to first grade from there. We still had to drive Joan to Bible Baptist Kindergarten. Thankfully, we had a carpool.

While getting Joan ready to start school, we discovered she had hearing loss which resulted in her having tubes put in her ears. When it came time to remove them, I was going to help. Being a nurse, I should be able to do that. Not so much. I almost passed out and had to go out of the room and sit down. Poor Joan had pain she didn't understand, and Mother was not there. It's different when it's your own child than when one is employed as a nurse and doing a job.

After Nancy was born, the doctor had put me on birth control pills because he thought I was not in good enough shape to handle another pregnancy. When we moved, I didn't think about getting a prescription to take along. When I ran out, I just went without. Soon I was pregnant again. When the doctor told me, "Yes, you are pregnant," I cried. I was afraid, and we didn't have money or insurance. I got used to the idea. Labor was easy. I didn't think we needed to hurry to the hospital, but when we got there, they rushed me to labor and delivery. Fifteen minutes later, with nothing for pain, I easily delivered a healthy baby girl. I have said, "It's a good thing they weren't all that easy or I would have had a dozen." I know now that it was God's plan. His plan is better than ours. Sandy has been a blessing all along. She was a good kid and has always been an encouragement to me.

That was August; the temperatures were up in the nineties. The air was dry so we didn't feel the temperature as much and didn't suffer from the heat.

15

By then, we had also discovered my favorite place in the world: Crater Lake. It was up in the mountains. At the entrance to the park was a gully. In it was what looked like pipes of steam coming up. I learned that was because the ground water was very warm and the steam had to come out. In fact, the whole town of Klamath Falls was heated with ground water keeping frost off the streets. When we got into the park, I was amazed to see a lake that was formed in the cavity of an inactive volcano. Somehow the top had fallen in and made an island in the lake. The sides of the lake were very steep. A road encircled the entire lake so we could get views from many directions. It had waterfalls, wildlife, including deer and antelope. We never saw any bears but heard they were there too. We even found snow in July. The girls got out of the car and made snowballs. It was a nice drive for a Sunday after church. Sometimes we took a picnic and could still be back in time for bed. One winter, we made it there to find the snow was deeper than the buildings, and they actually had a tunnel through the snow into the lodge. The big equipment had cleared the path and huge snowblowers moved the snow away. It seemed like we were driving in a narrow gully as we approached the top edge of the lake from the piles of snow two or three times higher than the car.

The ride there was also enjoyable. Along the way was quiet, peaceful Klamath Lake. The rock walls had rock slides like I had never seen in Michigan. About halfway was a small village called Chiloquin. Even though the village was off to the side of the road, one could see many small houses where Native Americans lived. Across the road from the village was a railroad track and the remains of a depot from days gone by.

Another place we liked to go was Lake of the Woods. One winter, we went there when the lake was frozen and people were fishing on it. Parking was near the lake, so it was easy to get to the lake with small children. It was a good day for fishing. If I remember correctly, Susan even pulled up a few fish. We went home with more than enough fish for a good meal. I think they were lake perch. The park had a nice shaded picnic area. The trees were mostly ponderosa pine. Most were very tall and straight. We were told that many of the trees were large enough to get lumber for a three-bedroom house from just one ie lumber from just one tree for a three-bedroom house.

Klamath Falls had a lumber mill where the logs from the mountains were milled into boards. Some logs were floated on the lake, and many were hauled in by truck. Some of the mountain roads were lumber roads. We explored a few. One of our favorite things to do in the evening was go to the mill parking lot after they were closed and watch the pelicans dive in the water, catch fish, and fill their pouches.

I never did figure where the waterfall was that Klamath Falls was named after. Perhaps it had been capped to make power for the city? Thirty miles south was the California border. We could see Shasta Mountain, California, from our house. It was snowcapped most of the year.

That part of Northern California was mostly fields and grazing land. The Air Force had a base and airport there with jet planes going in and out. Occasionally, we would hear the sonic booms of jets breaking the sound barrier as they took off. Also, a college was nested in the hills on the Oregon side: Oregon Technical Institute. At their front gate, they had a ring and parts that were from when the Japanese tried sending bombs by balloon to hit the US. Also south and up in the mountain high desert, we saw a hideaway for some pirate. I think they called it Captain Jack's Hideaway. We went there with Pauline and Jack Hert and all our kids but didn't dare get out of the car due to warnings about rattlesnakes. The place looked like high desert with lots of large rocks and short bushes.

What else do I remember? I go back to after Sandy was born. The washer broke. I washed diapers by hand and hung them on the line. Roger's mom came by train to visit. My parents and little brother John came to visit also by train. Judy came to visit. She drove all the way. As did Betty and Leonard later. Betty said that she was miserable all the way. We all guessed she might be expecting. The trip was the only time my dad was out of Michigan with the exception of the Canadian train trip he and Mom took later.

Even the dog was a helper. One day, we went into another room and left baby Sandy on the couch thinking she couldn't roll over. On returning, there was the dog up against the couch keeping Sandy from falling.

During this time, my sister Betty was getting married. She wanted Susan to be a flower girl and me to be a bridesmaid. When Judy came to visit, she brought lush burgundy velvet for dresses. I got to sew them. We made arrangements to go to Michigan to the wedding. That turned out to be a fun adventure. We took a train from Reno, Nevada, to Chicago and were picked up in Chicago. Sandy was only about six or eight months old. Disposable diapers were just on the market and came in handy on the trip. We switched her formula to powdered milk to make it easier to keep. The train seats reclined, so we slept on them. We all enjoyed the trip seeing the country out the window of the train. I think we stayed at Judy's when we got there. I think she had Matt then; he was just new. We enjoyed our great adventure. When we got back home, life went back to normal.

It must have been about then when Roger started drinking. The first time I noticed it is one day, he came home from the car dealership. He got on the little tricycle in the yard. With his legs over the top of the handle bars he peddled around the yard singing at the top of his voice. After that, he brought home a six-pack of beer daily and mostly consumed it that same night. It seems they often had a few drinks after work. Before that, Roger never came home with evidence of any alcohol.

Before we were married, he had sworn that he never would drink like his uncle or his dad. Though on rare occasions, he would have a beer. A little at a time, life changed after that. Roger used to play with the kids in the evening, or we would do something as a family. He became more and more distant and grumpier as time went on, verbal abuse was common.

One day, Roger came home and said we were moving. Roger had found us a house on Union Street. I wanted to go see it. He said that it was a done deal, so we would just move. He did end up taking me there a bit before we moved. It was a more up-to-date three-bedroom ranch. I am not sure why he wanted to move. Because I liked our house and was just getting to know the neighbors. The new house didn't have a garden space. The one good thing, we were closer to Susan's school. She had to walk a couple blocks to school. She still remembers how scared she was to cross a busy street.

After we moved, the dog disappeared. One day, he ran out when we opened the door and never came back. We tried to find him but with no luck. That was a very sad day for us all.

We were only a couple blocks from the store. I could take the kids in the wagon. I can't remember how it worked with four kids. Somehow it did, and we brought home whatever groceries we needed.

Susan got a bike. She would ride it to her dad's car lot. He had left the dealership and was managing a used car lot. Her dad paid her one cent each to pick up cigarette butts off the ground. She became Daddy's helper along with entertaining her sisters at home. Our house was across from the Armory. Most of the time, it was quiet there, but once a month, the reserves came for training. It was fun to watch the trucks and see what they did. One mildly windy day, when they were not there, looking out the window, I saw a mini tornado lift the cover off their trash can next to the building. It whirled the contents into the air and beyond. It looked like a mini tornado. I was told later that it was a whirly gig, and they were common in that area. It seems they were harmless to humans, but I wasn't so sure.

The Herts had become our best friends. They all enjoyed the out of doors as we did. Their Susan was less than a year older than our Susan. They played well together. Their two boys were a little younger. Darrel was about Joan's age. When there was a total lunar eclipse, they came over, and we watched it out of our windows. Trees blocked the view from their house, but we had a perfect view. It was the first time any of us had seen the shadow of the earth completely block out the moon then recede, letting us see the full moon again. We were all amazed.

One time, we went to the Herts' house for a birthday party. Pauline had made a birthday cake and set it on a shelf in their backroom for safekeeping. Nancy was maybe three or four. She had disappeared. We found her in the backroom. She had eaten a couple decorations off the cake and was licking some of the frosting off her fingers. Oh, was Pauline mad. She scolded Nancy severely. I don't think either of them ever forgot that. I felt bad for not watching Nancy closer. Even so, we still were fast friends and did things together.

Nancy was also getting into trouble because she sat so close to the TV. We also thought it was cute that she would crawl around on her hands and knees with her face maybe six inches from the ground and find the teeniest bugs. When she started Bible Baptist Kindergarten, she did not do as well as the others. We finally got her eyes tested. It turned out she was very nearsighted. She got thick Coke-bottle lenses in her glasses. Perhaps the nearsightedness was a result of having 100 percent oxygen as a baby. I had tears running down my face when we came outside from the eye doctor, after she said, "I can see that tree way over there." It was a half block away. If I hadn't been so vain, I think it may have been best for her if we had had her repeat kindergarten. About that same time, Joan got glasses.

By then, Roger was drinking more, and I was getting nervous. I started thinking I should be nearer to family if something happened. So I began complaining that I was homesick. We decided to move back to Michigan to be near family. Roger and Jack built us a trailer to haul our belongings in.

16

The trip back to Michigan in June was an adventure. We had packed everything we could take into the trailer. Roger was creative. The station wagon that pulled the trailer had been converted into a camper of sorts. Two of the girls would sleep on the two bench seats. The other two in the back with Roger and I on a mattress on the floor in the back of the station wagon. The mattress hung out the tailgate and a little beyond. So Roger had rigged a convertible tent with a tarp over the end. I remember one night, it was rainy and very cold. Thankfully, we had plenty of blankets.

The trip was basically uneventful except that we got a flat tire in Illinois. I think on the trailer we had no spare. Of course, it was in the evening, and we were in the country with no service stations nearby. We were forced to drive a distance on that flat tire. Finally, we found a small truck stop but had to wait until morning for them to fix the tire. I was all upset, but Roger kept his cool. Now where would we sleep? We must have looked like a family of gypsies about then. I guess we were. The truck stop people let us park behind their building to sleep. They must have wanted us out of there because in the morning, it wasn't long until the tire was fixed, and we were on our way.

I don't remember the rest of the trip. Judy had invited us to stay with her, so we stayed in her basement for six weeks. Some things I remember from there. Judy had a pregnant single girl living with her. Judy worked the night shift, so we tried to be as quiet as we could when Judy needed to sleep. We would get out of the house whenever possible. Just walking to the store and around the neighborhood helped pass some time. Once when Roger was gone, she loaned us her car so we all, including the expectant mom, piled in Judy's car. We headed out to check out yard and garage sales. We had seen a large sale advertised out in the country, so we headed out maybe ten miles from town. While we were at the sale, it started raining. Soon it was thunder and lightning. The wind blew really hard. The people that had come to the sale, including six of us, all packed inside the garage. The rain was coming down in heavy sheets. The owners closed the garage securely. We huddled in the garage. I began to think the garage would blow over. Tree limbs hit it and piled against it. As quick as it came, it let up. When we went outside, we were shocked to see trees down and branches everywhere. I couldn't believe the sun was already shining.

I don't remember buying anything. I think the expectant mom bought a couple baby things. We got in the car and headed back to Judy's. As I drove, we could see trees down all along the way, and sometimes we had to go around branches on the road. My foot was shaking on the gas pedal. I can't remember being so scared, and to myself I prayed, *God, please get us back safe.* As we got further along the same road I had traveled many times in years past, there were power lines down. From some, we could see live electricity shooting into the ground. Then I prayed, *Please don't let there be any wires on the road.* We had to go around some branches but made it home okay. I don't remember ever shaking so badly in my entire life. I had valuable treasure in that car: my four children and an expectant mom, with an unborn child.

Another thing I remember at Judy's is refinishing an old wooden rocker that Judy had found somewhere. She had gotten an antiquing kit on sale and encouraged us to redo the chair. To me, the paint looked like ugly dirty green, but Judy had said she bought it for us and at that time it was on sale. I thought, *Beggars can't be choosers.* Besides, it was supposed to be the fashion of the day. So with her help, we put the chair out on her driveway, stripped, scrapped, and sanded that chair until it was good according to the directions. Then carefully applied the antiquing. I have to admit, it turned out very nice to my surprise. I still have that chair today, just not green. Some look at it and drool like they wish they had it.

17

We stayed in Judy's basement for six weeks while Roger looked for, then found part-time work with Lewis Johnson, son of one of the builders that Roger worked for in the past. Lewis had a house on Comstock that we could buy on land contract with no down payment. It was across the street from the school. The house was a bit wonky in that it sat crooked on the one-acre lot and had a side door near the bedrooms that we didn't need or use. It had two bedrooms where we put a double set of bunk beds to accommodate the four girls in one room. Roger and I had the other bedroom. The house also had a sufficient living room with a nice picture window that let in a lot of light, a decent kitchen with room to put the table in the center, and of course, one bathroom. The basement had space for laundry and storage. Judy helped us find furniture to fill in what we didn't have in the trailer from Oregon. It wasn't long until we made a play area in the basement, then a sewing area down there. I remember the kids playing while Pat Newton and I made choir robes for the church. We still belonged to the Lutheran church.

At first, Roger tried to work enough to support us. He was an expert carpenter, and he could paint houses inside and out. But in the off season, there was no work. I remember being upset because we went to see if we could get some help. What happened greatly upset me. We were told we had two cars, so they could not help us. One was the old station wagon we brought from Oregon. The other was a few years old used van Roger was using for work. If he found any work, he needed the van for hauling. It didn't have back seats, so it wouldn't work for a family car. What to do? If I remember correctly, I found work at a nursing home part-time then full-time. I think I worked on the night shift. It worked because I could get the kids off to school and sleep until they got home, then take a nap before I went to work. Roger was there with the kids at night. Sandy was not in school that first year, but my cousin a block away through the woods kept her so I could sleep. They had twin girls her age. They all went to kindergarten together the next year. In later years, I mentioned to Sandy that I was sorry that I worked so much when they were young. She replied, "But, Mom, you were always there for us." That was the advantage of working the night shift.

At that house, we had a cat. One night, I woke up to Joan yelling, "This cat is having her kittens in my bed." Sure enough, under her covers was a wiggly bunch of tiny wet kittens. The cat knew who to trust. That cat was amazing. Above the girls' bedroom, we kept hearing noises, like birds or squirrels were up there. Somehow, the cat climbed between the walls and went up there. If I remember correctly, she brought down a dead squirrel. We never heard the noise after that.

I don't know that it would have made a difference if I was home, but Roger gradually increased his drinking. I tried to spend more time with him, so we took square dance lessons. We had fun. I made Roger a western shirt and me a dress to match. Of course, I had to have the full petticoat. Lucky for me, someone who was no longer able to dance sold theirs to me real cheap. We were blessed to have Debbie, a neighbor high school girl who was an excellent babysitter. The girls seemed to look forward to her coming.

As time went on, Roger became more and more verbally abusive. One day, we had an argument; I don't know about what. He hit me and knocked me down. I remember saying, "If you ever do that again, I am leaving." After that, he pushed me around but never knocked me down. The verbal abuse just got worse the more he drank. If I remember correctly, he was up to a six-pack a day at home. He was not one for going to bars then. He started going out for lunch and began to have a couple beers at noon.

He wanted to build us a better house. I was content where we were, but perhaps my suggestions as to how we could make improvements was more than he wanted to think about. We got a couple acres from my dad on Lincoln Street. We, mostly Roger, built a nice three-bedroom ranch with a basement and a family room behind the attached garage on Lincoln Street. Now I felt spoiled because we had a bath and a half. We had no problem selling the house on Comstock.

If I remember correctly, when we moved there, Susan was in tenth grade, Joan in eighth in junior high, Nancy in sixth in Robinson elementary, and Sandy in third also Robinson elementary. The girls were growing too fast. Susan had a friend Bettina who was an exchange student from Germany. Joan liked the idea of being an exchange student, so Joan decided she wanted to be an exchange student too. We were unable to help her with money, and I didn't have time to help her. I was working full-time, and Roger spent his money on beer and cigarettes plus long lunches. We had no connections that we could influence to help her. Even though we told her we couldn't help, she found her way. She was able to convince the Lion's Club to send her even though they had not previously sent exchange students. So she went to Sweden for nine months. That was hard for a mom to let her precious daughter go. Even worse because we were so poor, we couldn't even afford to send money for a ticket to come home if she needed to. Trusting God was what I had to do. I had no other choice, so I prayed daily for her safety. The hardest part came when she needed dental work, and we couldn't help. It turned out, somehow, her Swedish parents were able to figure it out.

Roger was drinking more and not rational many times. One time, he came to me and wanted to buy expensive Christmas gifts for twin boys of a waitress where he hung out. I was so offended. He hadn't even been helping at home, and we didn't have gifts for our girls. At least he asked but was mad at me because I had responded angrily.

I was taking in sewing to help out. Then on a whim, it seemed to me that if I got a space in town, there would be more business at an easier-to-reach location. So I did. I rented a storefront and scraped together fixtures where I could and took in handmade consignment items to have something in the showroom. Roger even made a big sign and put it up for me. Susan would walk from school to help. On weekends and vacations, sometimes, I would bring Nancy and Sandy with me. After about a year, it seemed to be getting off the ground. I was enjoying it.

However, one summer day, the kids at home called to tell me the dog had ran out on the road and was killed. Of course, they were crying. That did it. I couldn't bear to leave them at home by themselves. I closed the shop doors, notified the consignment people to pick up their things, and stayed home with the kids.

Desperate, I found a job working the night shift at a Mercy Hospital in Muskegon. I got to work in CCU (Cardiac Care Unit). Roger would be home at night. I paid the house payment, utilities, and bought groceries. There was little left for anything else. Roger worked when he could, but most of his money went for beer and cigarettes and whatever else he wanted. He often worked in the morning then went to lunch, had a couple beers, and didn't go back to work in the afternoon.

It was really hard when I had saved up nearly enough for the house payment in the checking account. He came home with a nice fourteen-foot runabout boat so he could go fishing. When I asked him where he got it, he said that he bought it. There was enough money in the checking account to make the down payment. It hadn't occurred to him that is was the money for the house payment. I remember thinking, *Okay, I earned the money for that boat. I will enjoy it too.* So as irresponsible as it was, whenever I could, I went fishing with him. I admit it was a good time and the girls were getting bigger or they were all in school, so it was easier to leave them. I worked the night shift and was tired all the time.

About then, Sue was dating Paul, Joan was in Sweden; Nancy was thinking, "Sue had Paul and choir, Joan went to Sweden, what can I do that's my own thing?" She never did realize how good she was on the clarinet and how proud of her I was. I went to football games just to see her in marching band. Sandy and I were becoming buddies as the other kids were busy doing their own thing.

18

I was content where we lived, but Roger wanted to build another house. He seemed to think that he could build it then sell ours or the new one and make money. The bank gave him a builder's loan. He found a lot in Dermshire Forest and went ahead to build a split-level house with a bed and bath down and three bedrooms and bath up. The main floor had a dream kitchen and nice living room. When it was finished, neither house sold. Finally, a family who had lost their house in a fire needed a place to live. They were willing to rent the Lincoln Street house until they had a new house built on their land. We moved into our new house. When the renters rebuilt, we sold the house on Lincoln Street and continued to live on Harry Street in Dermshire. While we were there, Joan came back from Sweden. Sue married Paul, the boy across the street, whom she had been dating even before the move. Nancy went to college and, in summer, to Cedar Point where she worked for a summer. Sandy was in high school and went to modeling school. It appeared to be the American dream, but all was not well in paradise. Roger was getting more and more verbally abusive. I worked the night shift, and he started going out at night.

Things went from bad to worse. One time, I went to pick Sandy up from school, but at the school, the car wouldn't start. I called him for help, but even though he was home doing nothing, he said things like, "If you had a brain, you'd be dangerous," and other profanities. He refused to come to help us. Having no money or road service, Sandy and I walked the five miles home. He must have felt guilty because he did finally come to help but did not see us walking. Thus he had more reason to blow up.

Joan came home from Sweden, and Sue and Paul got married. By then, I was so messed up, I don't remember the wedding, but I do remember that Sue made Paul's tux and her own dress. The bridesmaids wore pretty yellow sheer printed, handmade dresses.

Joan met Gary, and they got married. The only thing that I remember is that we had the reception at the Catholic Church hall. Roger had to have beer there. Sandy drank and ended up on her knees in front of the toilet in the bathroom. As far as I know, that was the last of her drinking. I think the bridesmaids dresses were blue.

Not long after that, my brother John got married. My memories of that were Roger drinking too much and not wanting to dance with me. But he danced with someone else, and she spread her legs enough to rub her bottom up and down on his leg. He let her do it and seemed to enjoy and encourage it. I started feeling sick even though I wasn't drinking. So when my mother was leaving, I asked her to take me home.

I didn't know what to do. I was praying and searching the Bible for answers. Things did not seem to be working out for good. I found Philippians 4:13, "I can do all things through Christ which strengthens me." This became my hope. I realized I needed to depend on Jesus.

I also looked up the verse I had depended on. Romans 8:28, "All things work together for good." I had never gone beyond that. It continued, "To them that loved God to them that are called according to His purpose."

I had to do some soul searching. *Did I really love God? Was I called according to his purpose?* I went through the Ten Commandments. I thought I did pretty good on the first nine, not perfect. Then I got to ten, "Thou shalt not covet." I wasn't sure about the meaning of covet, so I got a dictionary. I found "to want something that someone else has" or "to long for with envy." I found myself guilty. I did pray for forgiveness. I was always wishing I had things better, and when someone else got something good, I thought it should be me. I was jealous. Nothing was ever good enough for me.

Once I cooked a meal and Roger didn't like it. In front of the kids all around the table, he threw it at me. By then, I had learned there was a place to call that helped women, Women in Transition. I called them right then. They helped me calm down and set an appointment for counseling. The first counselor and I didn't connect, but the second one had lived with an alcoholic father. She understood.

I started responding less to the abuse. I gave up picking up Roger's beer cans and, in fact, started making a pyramid with them. It often got big enough to cover the end table where they sat before he would take them to recycle for more beer money. I quit opening bills addressed to him unless it was a utility bill or something I wanted to pay to keep us going. It got so I started thinking he was the bill collector due to the piles of mail that he didn't open. If I knew the house was already clean and Roger came home and started his hollering, I would simply not let it bother me and didn't cry about it like I used to. Sadly, he started in on the girls. And Nancy seemed to get the worst of it. I did notice that when he came home, the girls all scattered to their rooms or anywhere to be out of the way.

After all the trying to be good and the hard work I tried to put in, including paying the house payment and bills and trying to keep things up at home, the girls were all working or gone. One day, Roger took me out to a nice dinner. I had hope of making a new start. Instead, he told me he didn't want to be married anymore. We danced and hugged. I cried. When we went home, I moved into an empty bedroom. He had the lower level. Sandy and I were upstairs. Nancy was working at Cedar Point. He had to come up for meals. I tried to do that for six weeks and only got an ulcer, with bad stomach pains. The doctor prescribed medicine that helped. It was then that I decided to move out. I talked to Nancy at Cedar Point and Sandy at home, and they seemed to think it was a good idea.

19

So I found an upstairs apartment above a business in Center Town. I could walk to work from there and save gas. I could walk to the waterfront to relax, and at night, I could hear the music from the musical fountain. It was summer, so it was a nice place to be. Sandy could walk to high school. I was working the night shift.

Sandy graduated the next year. We were poor. I wanted to make her a prom dress, but she was invited but decided not to go. I think she did not want to put me through more and I felt bad.

To this day, I regret leaving pictures and the like behind. Maybe I was hoping Roger would change his mind.

People that had been friends with Roger thought I was terrible. So did my two married daughters and their husbands. I always said that Roger was a nice guy when he wasn't drinking. That was first thing in the morning. He usually started at noon, and it went from bad to worse then. People told me they thought he was a nice guy, but they didn't know how it was at home.

Hanging on to hope that we could reconcile, I went to the pastor for help, but he just made me feel worse. I continued on. In the fall, I went to talk to Roger. He had guys working with him in the garage. But he went in the house with me and took me into the bedroom. He said that we were still married, so it was okay. I hoped that it meant that it would work out with us. After that, we talked. He didn't want a divorce. He didn't think the drinking was a problem and didn't want to change anything, but I could move back and clean and cook if I needed a place to stay.

Shortly after, one late afternoon, I went for a very long walk. I walked all over Grand Haven. I even walked through the cemetery. It was a moonlit night. The shadows and gravestones were there, but I didn't pay attention to them. I was talking to God, telling him that I was disappointed that he didn't help us keep things together. When I got married, it was for the rest of my life. I cried hard. I think I hoped in the cemetery no one would hear me. I told God in no uncertain terms how mad I was at him for letting things fall apart. There were very few streets I didn't walk that night.

I realized it was getting late, but I had five dollars in my pocket. I thought, *I have tried to be good all my life, but it didn't work. Maybe I missed some fun too. So I will go to the bar near my apartment and use the money to get drunk. If that isn't enough, some guy will likely buy me more from what I have heard. If a man takes advantage of me, I don't care. Being good hasn't worked. I just give up.*

As I neared home and was about to cross the street to the bar, my sister Betty and her husband stopped in front of me and said, "What are you doing here at this time of night?"

I said, "I went for a walk. What are you doing here?" I knew they lived a good ten miles out of town.

They responded, "We were thinking about you and decided to come and see if you were all right."

Light bulb. *Oh my gosh! What did I almost do?* They had just saved me. Why were they there at that exact time and place? It had to be God's doing. I thought, *Praise the Lord.* Right then, I knew he sent them to save me from myself.

At some point, I talked to Roger. He told me, "I found someone I can love, and you should too."

Soon my paycheck was garnished for Roger's bills. Not knowing what to do, I went to a lawyer. The lawyer said that the only way to stop this from happening again was to file for divorce. So I did.

Sundays were very lonely, no one wanted to spend time with this terrible person who left her husband. I kept hearing about the singles group that met on Sunday afternoons. I thought, *That might be a good place to meet other women who were lonely too.* So I tried it. I found they had a topic for study at every meeting. Usually something for self-help. So I decided, *If nothing else, I need that.* I met a couple women who had been there longer than myself. They invited me to go with them to dances and other events sponsored by the group. I started going with them as often as I could to relieve some of the loneliness.

Soon a quiet guy asked if he could ride with us to Muskegon to a dance. He said that he didn't think his old truck would get him there. With three girls in the car, it seemed pretty safe. The first time, we took my car. He left his old truck at my house. Funny thing, the next day, he came back and said that he had left his shoes in my car. He came in, we visited for a short time. He went with the girls and myself a couple more times and stopped to visit once or twice.

About the same time, my daughter gave birth to their first child in Indiana. I wanted to go see my grandson. But I didn't want to drive by myself. This guy seemed safe enough, so I asked him to go with me to drive. I would pay him. He agreed. My daughter and her husband thought he was strange and didn't seem to believe that the guy was no more than a friend helping me out. As quiet as he was, they thought the situation a bit strange. After that, he came to my apartment a few times. We teased a bit but nothing happened. It seemed fun to have someone around.

One day, he came over with binoculars and made like he was trying to see something out the window. He also made a point of telling me directions to where he lived. I didn't see him for a couple days then realized he had left the binoculars on a windowsill behind a curtain in my apartment. I waited a couple more days then decided to return them.

PART 3
Still Spoiled: God Is Good

20

It was a lovey early spring day in May. The white trees were blooming, the ones that bloom before the dogwood. I liked what I saw along the way through Spring Lake and on to a mile before Fruitport.

When I arrived, I saw his old green pickup truck and a shiny yellow one. Behind them, I saw an old shack with faded blue paint that looked like it could have been a chicken coop at one time. Beside it was a little red barn in need of repair. I hesitated going to the door but thought, *What have I got to lose?* I knocked. A guy that I had seen come to the singles only once with Al answered the door.

He looked at me with a big smile and said, "How may I help you?" When I asked if Al was there, he looked to his right and said, "Al, someone is here to see you." Al didn't come to the door. So the guy asked me, "Is there something I can help you with?"

I said, "I am returning the binoculars that Al left at my place." The guy invited me in. Hesitating with one step inside the door, I saw Al sitting on a couch with a couple kids.

The guy said, "Al, are you going to talk to her? If not, I will." Al didn't move.

The new guy said, "It looks like Al doesn't want to talk. I would like to talk to you, but it's hard to talk here. Can we go someplace where we can talk?"

I handed him the binoculars and said, "I guess."

He said, "You might feel more comfortable if we took your car. Is that okay?"

I was hesitant but didn't much care what happened to me about then, so I said, "Yes, but I don't have much time. I need to get home and take a nap because I have to work tonight."

"I know a place close by where it will be easy to talk."

We got in my car, and I drove to where he directed. It was nearby on a dirt road off the main road where no one traveled. I thought, *This does not look good. What did I get myself into?* Because I was leery of his motives, I sat with my back to the door.

He said, "My name is Chuck." He proceeded to ask me about me and told me a little about him. At one point, he tried to hug me, maybe because he could see that I was trying not to cry. Not trusting him, I pushed him away.

Then he said, "I'd like to talk more, could we meet at a restaurant sometime?"

I said, "I sleep most days and work nights, so it is hard to do that. But I always eat breakfast at home after work. You could come and have breakfast with me." I felt safe doing that because Sandy was there.

Believe it or not, he was there the next morning when I got home from work. I started to fix bacon and eggs. He started to tell me how to cook eggs, so I handed him the spatula and said, "You do it then." He did, then proceeded to tell me how he thought eggs should be cooked according to his experience.

After that day, he was there most every day. We consumed pots of coffee and talked about everything we could think of. I found out he had three children. He told me his ex-wife was in a mental hospital, that he still cared about her, but divorced in order to get help to care for the children. He told me he had gone to see about getting help to care for the children so he could work. He was told that because he was still married, they couldn't help him even though she hadn't been there for some time. At that, he immediately went to file for divorce. No problem getting help then.

He was a good listener and let me unload on him. I needed that. As hard as it was, many times I had to kick him out because I had to sleep or go to work. At first, I tried to get rid of him or at least come over less, but nothing I said or did convinced him to back off a bit. One evening, we kissed good night. He walked out like he was walking on a cloud. I think he knew he had won me over. Not that he had to try very hard.

Soon he brought his kids to meet me one at a time. I remember the first one that came opened my refrigerator and said, "Food." The kids, being young teens, seemed to like to come, so they could walk down town and hang out. Chuck and I would talk until I had to go to work. Some days, it was hard to get him to leave. For a treat, we would occasionally go for coffee or dessert at the Rendezvous but seldom went on regular dates. We just talked and talked and talked and drank lots of coffee. We seemed to have a mutual attraction.

Somewhere along the way, Al was gone. Now I wonder, *Was he sent by God to connect Chuck and I?*

One of the sweetest memories of that time is the day Chuck invited me over for dinner. His oldest daughter Laurie had cooked us a nice chicken dinner with all the fixings. It was a hot day. Laurie looked hot and tired. I offered to do the dishes. She was happy to go and lie down. They didn't have hot water, so we had to heat water on the gas stove. I had never used gas, so I was afraid of it. Chuck was happy to show me how. He couldn't get over the mountain I could make on the dish drainer.

Soon things started happening way too fast. I told him if we went too far, he would have to marry me. He didn't seem to care. Maybe we were both too lonely and starved for affection. He told me he and the kids needed me. I needed to be needed. Soon we went too far after he assured me he had a vasectomy and I couldn't get pregnant. We then planned to be married around our birthdays in

THE LIFE OF A SPOILED BRAT

August. I prayed a lot because things seemed so crazy, but the voice in my head said, *Marry him*. Repeatedly, I argued with myself. He only has that old shack and not enough room. He's gone a lot on the trucks, but *I am ruined anyway, so I may as well go ahead with it. Anyway, it's obvious they need a woman in the house.*

Laurie had been the woman of the house. She seemed to be able to handle Linda and Roger just fine. Chuck said that it wasn't fair that she had to take so much responsibility. At that time, Chuck was driving semi to support them.

Since we were acting like we were married anyway, I moved in with him and his three kids. He said he needed me and the kids needed me. I needed to be needed. That didn't make it right, and I knew it. I prayed hard. Something kept telling me, *It's okay*. As I look back, Chuck and I were acting like a couple crazy teenagers. When my advance rent payments ran out, Sandy and Nancy would move in with us. *Where would we all fit in that little chicken coop?* Three and a half months after I first met Chuck, we were married at his church with two witnesses. We had started attending church there regularly.

This after I had considered what it would be like to live in a converted chicken coop with a bunch of teenaged kids. The chicken coop had a nearly flat roof. Plus everything on the floor inside rolled one way. We had running water and two bedrooms and one bath. Chuck was proud of the water heater he had installed for me.

We wanted our anniversary to be near our birthdays so we would only have to celebrate once. We took the twenty-seventh of August because it was the closest the pastor had available. I wore a new cream-colored knee-length dress. Chuck wore a blue shirt and tie. His friends were our witnesses. Linda and Roger were the only guests. We didn't tell anyone else for fear they wouldn't approve. The day we got married, I had to work that night. So we did not have a honeymoon.

When we got home after the quiet wedding, I went in the house first. I couldn't believe what I saw in the living area to my left of the door. In the middle of the floor stood a white see-through person. Like a cloud in the shape of a person. She had her arms crossed and a very stern look on her face. I took a second look, and sure enough, she was there. In my mind, I said, *Who are you?* In my mind, she responded, *I am Chuck's deceased mother, and you had better be good to him.* Then she was gone. I tried to pretend it didn't bother me. I knew I would be good to him. The question really was, would he be good to me? I figured I was taking a big risk. I saw her several times as the days and months passed, always in the same spot. She gradually let her arms relax and her face gradually became calm, no longer stern. Mostly, she just watched. *Was I going off the deep end?*

A few years later, we were in our new house. There she was at the end of the kitchen near the door. As soon as she saw me notice her, she started dancing in a happy kind of dance, jumping up and down. I felt she was saying, "At last, I know Chuck will be okay. I can move on." It has me wondering if God allows people to stay until they see that their children are okay. You all will say no, it's my imagination, but it seemed so real.

THE LIFE OF A SPOILED BRAT

After the wedding, my married daughters and their husbands thought I had gone off the deep end. Perhaps I had, but I kept praying for God to direct me. Things seemed to be working as far as I could see. Except that my married kids didn't want anything to do with me. As I look back from what they could see and what they heard from the rumor mill, I looked pretty bad. Chuck did have a past, but he let that all go when he met me. I resent the rumors that made our life difficult. As I look back, when he met me, Chuck started setting his life in order. The past was gone. I was beside myself with grief over not seeing my daughters and begged to meet with all of them. I tried to plead my case. They weren't convinced. The sons-in-law told me that I was unfit to be a grandmother. Those were the most painful words I ever heard, even worse than having one's husband say he didn't want to be married anymore.

Perhaps I had gone off the deep end because things no one could believe happened to me. Like the night I was working in intensive care. A patient was apparently breathing her last. A code was called and all efforts were made to revive her. At the very moment the monitor showed a flat line, I blinked, and in that short instant, I saw what appeared to be a mist going straight up from her. I have tried to find a reason for this, but the only thing I can think is her spirit left her body at that very instant, and I saw it.

I worked the night shift at the local hospital until they laid off the LPNs about a year later. I didn't know what to do as hospitals were laying off most LPNs in the area. I took in sewing at home and did dressmaking for a few people, but the space in our house was very small.

By then, Chuck had given up truck driving because he said that he wanted to "stay married." He had started an upholstery course, studying on his downtime while truck driving. He started doing upholstering in the middle of our tiny living room. When he decided upholstering was what he wanted to do, he built a garage big enough for a workshop and a car. It was only ten steps from the house. It gave him a much better place to work. The garage was large enough that he sectioned off a sleeping room for two girls. I would like to add that he asked me if it was okay to do upholstery and to build a garage. I was happy to have him home and then to have more space in the house.

21

Sometime along the way, the house roof leaked, and we actually put a plastic sheet over our bed so we could stay dry while we slept. Chuck had repaired the roof a few times, but the flat roof wouldn't stay fixed. Once I went to take a bath. I filled the old clawfoot tub and got in looking forward to a nice soothing soak. The tub started tipping; in a panic, I jumped out. I was sure the tub was going through the floor. A tub leg had gone through the old board floor just that quick. That was sure scary.

When Chuck removed the tub and started tearing out the old rotten boards, he found that termites had eaten through the boards and had nearly eaten through the joist under there. How long would it be until the joist gave way and the whole house caved in? I insisted that we build a new house.

Chuck had tried to get a building permit previously, but we couldn't tear down the old house first because we still needed a place to live. For lack of money, we couldn't see our way to renting another place until a new house was done. We were desperate. We made ourselves a bedroom in the new garage. By then, Laurie had moved out, and Roger was mad at his dad and left. Nancy was in California. Sandy and Linda had the bedroom in the garage, and Chuck and I moved our bed into the main workshop and shared it with the upholstery. It maybe was ten steps to the old house, so we even walked through snow that winter to go to the bathroom. A couple times, we used the bathroom and a mama raccoon and her babies were actually in the bathroom with us. I admit that shook me up. Can you imagine me sitting with my feet up on the toilet seat watching the cute little critters scurry around to find food? Finding nothing, they left, but I can't imagine anyone having an experience like that ever.

We had gotten blueprints for the house we liked. Put it on the wall to remind us what we were working for. People didn't believe we could ever do it. They were so used to seeing us do without. At one time, Chuck tried to get a variation to live in the old house while we built the new one, but the township board didn't allow it.

Changing that and getting the building permit was a blessing from God. The building inspector didn't seem to like Chuck, so I went to get the permit. The inspector was very busy and simply handed me the paperwork. I filled it out. He took my money and gave me the permit, with mine and Chuck's name on it. Chuck couldn't believe it. I still wonder what the building inspector thought when he realized it was for Chuck.

We started gathering up free or very low-cost materials. We even bought the contents of a builder's garage full of doors and all kinds of materials for a token price. All we had to do was empty his garage within a limited time. Also, a friend kept bringing us free leftover cement blocks and lumber too. Other friends helped us collect things, even good used carpet. We stored some in part of our garage and some on pallets under tarps in the yard. We owned the lot in front. Selling it provided money for most of what we needed. Chuck didn't want a basement due to the high water table, but he wanted an enclosed crawl space, so it had a cement floor and an extra block or two high to make it to his specifications.

On a couple days, friends and family helped with the construction. Even my ex-husband helped and supervised the foundation and the ruff-in construction. Our girls were there. They carried blocks to the guys that were laying them. They brought their little ones, and we had a picnic of sorts. After the foundation passed inspection, the subfloor was laid and outside walls went up. I actually laid out the floor plan according to the blueprint. We got the studs up for the walls.

We were blessed to get one thousand two hundred dollars from my mother's estate and used it for more of what we needed. We bought trusses, the easiest, fastest way to get the roof on. The house was enclosed. By then, we were out of money, and it was too cold to work inside that winter. So the house was on hold until spring.

It seems it was about then we had to give in and get a loan to finish the house. The bank was not willing to loan to us. But a loan shark with very high interest was happy to. Chuck and friends put up the drywall. He was having trouble reaching up and had gotten a rig to hold the drywall sheets up to the ceiling. In the end, my sister and I finished piecing in the dry wall. I did the mudding of seams. I think Chuck helped. The mud job was far from perfect, but it was done. Chuck had done the wiring and plumbing before the dry wall. We had invested every cent we could in the house. After we painted and moved in, we were able to get a bank loan and pay off the loan shark.

    We were proud and happy with our nice three-bedroom ranch house with one and three quarter's baths.

22

In the meantime, I had started a dress shop about three miles away on a main road. That's my next story.

I got laid off from nursing. I never dreamed nurses ever got laid off, but if you were an LPN, it happened. To do something, I decided to take in sewing. That was my first love anyway, and I had studied dress design many years ago. Anyway, I started sewing and alterations at home and was surprised at the demand. I had one problem. Chuck had the new garage for his upholstery, but there really was not a comfortable place to sew. Life seemed like one interruption after another.

One day, I got an impulse to take a different way home. About three miles from home on a busy road, I saw a little shop for rent. I kept thinking that could be a good place for a dress shop. I went back and got the phone number from the posting, called the landlord, and made an appointment to see it. I had no money to start a business. Not even enough to pay the first month's rent. I negotiated that I would pay one hundred dollars now and the rent plus the deposit in the first few months. The landlord took me at my word and let me rent.

It's amazing to me what one can do when they set their mind to it and God is in it. I advertised for consignment wedding and formal dresses with good response. We had a sheet of plywood that I had my husband saw into the shape of a woman with a very full skirt and painted it with letters large enough to be read from the road: Dream Gowns. I gathered tables and racks from wherever I could find them. Not having hanging racks enough, I bought plastic chain with large links and strung them up for hanging dresses on. Chuck built a cubicle for fitting room from paneling that we had in our garage. It may have come from the stuff we got from the builders garage that we didn't use for the house. The long mirror came from my previous life.

In the meantime, I kept sewing at home to take in money. I had to pay to have the power turned on but didn't get the phone or gas hooked up right away. It was late spring, so we could do without heat. The advertising was the sign and word of mouth. I actually made enough the first month to pay the rent and other bills.

It was amazing how easy it was to stock the store. Many people had dresses they used only once and were happy to find a market for. All it took was a tiny ad to get people to bring them for me to sell on consignment. Soon I found a supplier for discounted dresses, and the business grew quickly. Very soon, I was able to get a phone but waited to have the gas turned on until we needed it for heat in the fall. There seemed to be plenty of people who wanted alterations. Pants hems and fitting problems became my specialty. I could have kept going on just that. However, I loved to make things from scratch and was good at designing and fitting odd shapes. Making wedding gowns and bridesmaids dresses became my passion. Soon the sewing became more than I could handle, so I hired a girl to help me. She didn't know much about sewing, but she was easy to train. She wanted to learn and was a quick learner.

I enjoyed sewing and my shop. I met so many wonderful people. Prom season was fun. Girls were so excited to find used or new prom dresses at discounted prices. Some even came back later to find a wedding dress. The business wanted to grow, but not having business training, I didn't know how to grow it. The bookkeeping became a burden. My husband had been trying to get involved. We both had taken a bookkeeping course. He volunteered to help me, with pay of course. By then, he knew quite a bit about computers and was anxious to help out. I let him. Mistake. He seemed to think that the income was all profit. So we started to discuss what to do about it, and it became a wedge between us. Rather than split up with him, I gave up the business and went back to work as an LPN in a nursing home. As I think back, I wish I had stuck it out. But I didn't. Will always wonder if we could have made it work.

After seven years, I closed the shop and went to work at a nursing home. Those were hard years. I was frequently charge nurse and didn't like that there never seemed to be enough help to take care of people the way I would want my mother taken care of. The first place I worked was a distance away from home at Lamont, second shift.

One evening, I went to work. There was a blizzard. I remember the highway was snow-covered and blowing, so I opted to take the side roads home. As it was, they were so bad you could not even see the road. The snow had blown across and covered it. The one good thing, there was no traffic, so I could drive really slow and watch carefully in the headlights. My hands and feet were shaking. Thankfully, I had good windshield wipers. I made it home okay but didn't think I wanted to drive that far anymore.

That's when I decided to find a job closer to home. I did, but I still was not content with the ratio of help to patient care needs just as before. I was very uncomfortable being charge nurse. If something went wrong, it was on me, and all the lives were my responsibility. As it was, I tried four nursing homes to find what I thought was satisfactory but never did. It was a paycheck. Chuck was doing well at the upholstery. So finally, I gave up. I was having back and hip problems anyway. At about age sixty-one, I quit nursing.

I wrote to the state and the president to let them know that nursing homes needed more help. I even included a packet of things I had observed. At least I tried the best I knew how. Actually, the Michigan Legislature started a bill to require more help, but it didn't pass. Money, you know.

I was close to being able to collect social security and started to have more hip trouble. A good chiropractor really helped me. Finally, he insisted that I have hip surgery. With the urging of people and the chiropractor, I finally gave in to hip surgery. By then, people would look at me with much pity in their eyes. I couldn't bear to look at that. I ended up having both hips done within three months of each other. Then a year to recover. I was collecting social security by then, and Medicare paid for most of my hip surgery.

Chuck was doing okay with upholstery. He still liked to spend all he could. We refinanced the house a few times to catch up with the bills. He was a smoker and had tried many times to quit, but he said that it was like trying to quit heroin. Cigarettes took their toll on him and on the income.

Previous to that, Chuck tried many things to make a fortune. For example, Tupperware, Stanley products, Watkins, Pampered Chef, and even Prime America. A side note: I benefited from them all in that the overflow of products helped to stock our shelves. With Prime America, we took a trip to Atlanta with the group. Chuck's intentions were good but could never stick to anything long enough to make it pay. I tried to help him while wanting him to take responsibility. Upholstery was best. People liked his work and kept calling him. The demand wouldn't let him quit. He even recovered the seats for a few area McDonald's stores.

23

At one point, Roger moved out. The youngest and last to leave. He and his dad had words, so he walked away. He was stubborn; he could have come back anytime if he could get along with his dad. Rumor has it that he slept on the beach or under a bridge that summer, even on sympathetic friends' porches. He could have given in and come home and helped his dad once in a while. Roger worked at the Rendezvous mostly night shift as a server or cook. He really wanted to work at a Native American casino. A new one was opening in Battle Creek, so he went there. He was hired and there to help open the new casino.

Laurie and Doug had moved to Maine where his parents lived. He was an engineer. They had lived in Idaho for a while. Linda and Cliff moved to the UP after living near Tustin for a time and, before that, near colleges so Cliff could end up with a PhD then a fellowship in, I think, neuropsychology.

My girls were closer. Sue and Paul stayed in Grand Haven and had an excavating business. Joan and Gary moved with the Coast Guard and finally retired to Grand Haven where Gary works for the county and Joan works for Mercy Health. Nancy lives in Muskegon. She seems to love buying things and selling on the Internet. Sandy and Clay live near his parents in Norton Shores. He is a great tile setter. Of course, there are grandchildren and great grandchildren. I am blessed to hear from most of them and some are close.

Now I feel like Job in the Bible. In the end, he got back more than he had lost. One of the hardest things for me, way back when, was the kids, especially sons-in-law, didn't like the fact that I got divorced and remarried. Because the relationship went so fast, they told me to my face that I was not fit to be a grandmother. As a result, the pain led to hold back making an effort to spend time with the grandkids. It hurts, yet today, I understand where they were coming from. The gossip mill makes things seem worse than they really are. In the end, they turned around and respected me. To this day, I think that is all past.

Occasionally, Chuck and I took in homeless people. There was Eugene, Susie, Herb, and Joe. Eugene was a pleasure to have around and helped where he could. He and Chuck were both retired Navy, so they understood each other. Herb is one who brought us a bunch of building material. His favorite saying was, "Don't worry about it." We had Susie who had been to drug rehab. She did okay at first but got in with the old friends. Then one night, she disappeared and so did my prescription drugs. Later, she wanted to come back, but we didn't trust her. Then there was Joe, my daughter's husband, whom she found out couldn't live with her because she lived within one thousand feet from the school he had a record from long ago. (Young people, what you do today can mess up your future.) He agreed to pay Chuck three hundred a month rent. Most of the time, he would hand Chuck a small amount and have "more tomorrow." We started wondering which tomorrow he meant. Chuck wrote him receipts for everything he got. Nancy even paid for him sometimes. He was a mechanic. Chuck did deduct the work Joe did on the car for a regular rate from the rent. When we said that he could live with us, we didn't know a little dog came with him. But there she was.

Chuck didn't drink, but he sure did smoke. He tried to quit many times. Once, he quit for about twenty days and was doing well. Then one day, he got a call that his son Roger had been in an accident and was in the ICU. The first thing Chuck did was get a pack of cigarettes. He started up, never to quit again.

It was a long drive to Kalamazoo. Roger was unconscious for a few days and had a very high fever. They worked hard to keep his temperature down so it wouldn't fry his brain. The casino people were wonderful and helped us all they knew how. I think they even put us up in a hotel for a couple nights. It's kind of a blur. I do recall the first night they brought food for everyone at the hospital waiting room. The casino people crowded the waiting room with so many of them. We could only spend very limited time in the room with Roger.

We went to the hospital most every day for most of the time Roger was in that unit. It was a hard drive, but it was our kid. When Roger was conscious, he was belligerent and fought most of the treatment. Soon they transferred him to a rehab hospital in, I think, Plainwell, close to Kalamazoo. It was still a long drive. But we tried to be there for him most every day. Even kept a notebook for people to leave notes, and I used it as a journal. We later gave it to Roger. We watched Roger learn to talk, swallow food, and then feed himself. We watched him learn to walk where two people would go with him holding him up, teaching him to use a walker. One would move his legs while the other helped hold him up at the walker.

He was not a very cooperative patient. But they did a fantastic job with him anyway. Roger's mind thought he was as he used to be and thought they were restricting him. He wanted to fight. For our convenience, we had him moved to Mary Free Bed in Grand Rapids. We had heard about the wonders they did with patients. At first, they kept him in a unit where he had plenty of space to move around outside his room but did not have the freedom to go beyond that area unattended. At some point, they moved him to the next step where he would be in with other people in a similar situation. He was free to move about within the common area and seemed to like it. When they moved him to a less restricted area with a step up in rehab, they even had a kitchen where he could cook when he graduated to that. All he really wanted was to get his driver's license, but he was nowhere near ready for that. He didn't want to cook. He said that was their job. One time, he managed to get out of the building. Chuck got a call that they couldn't find him. It turns out, he was walking home. They found him a few blocks away.

When they told us they could do no more for him and wanted to transfer him to another home back near Kalamazoo, Roger and Chuck visited there, but Chuck was not comfortable with that. It seems it was near a highway, and Chuck was concerned that Roger would walk on to the highway and get hit by a car. We found a place in Whitehall that seemed a good fit.

At one point, we tried to keep Roger at home. It was working okay, until one day, Roger had gone to the store while we were at church. He got what he thought he wanted then went home and shut himself in his room and apparently drank until when he came out of the room he was hanging on to the walls. He couldn't stand up, then fell and hit his head. We had to take him to the emergency room. A couple other incidents, and we were convinced that we couldn't manage him.

Also, he was creating a wedge between Chuck and me. At one point, I was trying to convince Chuck that we couldn't manage Roger. Chuck ended up saying if I couldn't deal with Roger, I could just leave. That was the worst it ever got between us. The voice in my head said, *Just stick it out, it will be okay.*

After Chuck and Roger had a couple wrestling matches, Chuck finally realized that it was not going to work. Yes, Roger was strong, but Chuck was quicker and could outmaneuver him. Roger went to the place in Whitehall that dealt with others like Roger. They know what to do and have put up with him since. Chuck was still legal guardian.

But they were responsible for the care. Roger learned to ride a bike again and seemed to enjoy it. He quit when he realized someone would have to go with him all the time. He failed to look when crossing the street and had snuck out and gotten beer a couple times.

Shortly before Chuck died, he turned the guardianship over to a court appointed guardian. Chuck knew he was dying and unable to do the paperwork or deal with the issues.

24

Chuck was having much knee pain, then went to have knee surgery. While there, he learned that he had lung cancer and would likely die. He didn't want to tell me. Later, he told my daughter and said that he hadn't told me because he didn't want to see me cry. He apparently told Joan while she was at the hospital to visit. At home, he told me he had lung cancer and tried to be strong. He gave me hope that he thought a special diet would cure him. I think he didn't want me to think the cancer was as bad as it was. We went to the doctor. She said it might be time to bring in hospice. At that point, I wish I knew that it was really that bad. Chuck didn't want to admit it to me and denied needing hospice yet. He refinanced the house and paid the bills, made arrangements to have the court get a new guardian for Roger. I watched as he continued to get worse. As hard as he tried to be brave, we ended up getting a wheelchair. Finally, a special mattress and oxygen. I was helping him in and out of chairs. He still tried to give me hope. I had seen people with oxygen in wheelchairs that needed help live for years.

The final thing was the last straw. We went to the doctor. She said, "You will die from this." When I asked how long he might have, she said that she thought about one to three weeks. I still had hope for longer. We consented to hospice. It was good. They could get him stronger pain meds and were a great support and help for me. That day, we stopped at the tobacco store. He could barely walk, but he walked in and bought cigarettes. The next couple days were hard. He could barely light his cigs and feed himself. I wanted to help him. Finally, the last couple days, he let me.

One day, he wanted to go to bed to see if he could be more comfortable. He took a short nap. When he woke up, I was right there. He looked to his right. He couldn't talk but made it clear he wanted to get up and was working his way toward the edge of the bed. I told him to wait, I would bring the wheelchair. He motioned to me with his index finger to come there. I went. He grabbed me and hugged me so hard it hurt. When I said it hurt, he pushed me away, then started toward the edge of the bed. I said, "Wait, I will get the chair." I turned to get the chair at the foot of the bed. As I turned back, I saw him slumped over at the side of the bed, then slither like a snake off the edge of the bed. He was still breathing but not responding. I tried to put a pillow under his head. But couldn't. I called hospice for help to get him up from the floor. They said they would be there in twenty minutes or so. They had to come from Muskegon.

In the meantime, someone came to the door. He said he was the hospice chaplain and had come to visit with Chuck. I was so relieved to see him and explained what had just happened. He went with me to see Chuck who was still breathing shallow. In a short time, Chuck quit breathing. Did God send the chaplain right at that time to give me some peace? The hospice girls got there, and between the three of them, they got Chuck in bed. Of course, they had to call the coroner. One of them called him and answered a bunch of questions. Because Chuck was terminal, the coroner didn't need to come.

They called the mortuary, then cleaned Chuck up and put clean clothes on him. I found Chuck's favorite shirt and pants. Chuck had requested to be cremated. Even so, he left there dressed as he would any day. My last view of him was looking peaceful in bed, dressed in some of his favorite clothes. He looked like him, only an empty shell. I thought, *He's not there*. I cried hard when I saw him, knowing that would be the last time even though he wasn't in there anymore. I was losing my best friend. When the mortuary people got there, they asked me to step out of the room. The last thing I saw was a body bag being dragged out. They had to do that because the gurney didn't take the corners.

Previously, I told you that sometimes I had strange dreams. One more I had a few times was one where I was standing in a line waiting to go into a separate room. Across the room from where I was, Chuck was in another rather sparse line waiting to go through a door. He had already been to the room where I was going. Out of that same room down below, a crowded path of people were hurrying out of a different door away from the room. It seemed like everyone went in the same door and most people came out

THE LIFE OF A SPOILED BRAT

the lower door. Chuck had come out of a door higher up where very few people came from. I remember being mad at Chuck because he went ahead of me and was trying to tell him he was in the wrong line. He seemed very much at peace and shook his head like he knew he was in the right place.

I wonder if this was telling me that Chuck would die first and he would go to the higher place while most people would go the other route. I hope when my time comes, I follow Chuck. I never did care for crowds.

Why did Chuck hug me so hard? I think it was because he knew he was going. He had always said he wanted us to go together. He was trying to take me along. I imagined that he pushed me away because he was told or thought that he couldn't take me. I do believe he saw something that I did not see.

I feel comfortable that Chuck went to be with Jesus. I can still see him at his forever home running around, looking for everyone in the Bible asking them question after question. Those last weeks, I had seen a major change in him, a forgiveness and honesty that he had never shown before. He had spent years searching the Bible and asking questions of pastors.

We had been reading the Bible out loud together daily. Was it months or years before when I realized that he still wasn't sure about the Bible and forgiveness. I told him that if he would go to church regularly, I would go where he picked. He had tried a couple churches, and I was still at the same church. He hadn't been going with me. He tried a couple churches, then we tried together. He liked one, and we went to talk with the pastor with twenty questions in writing to be sure it was something we could believe. The capstone was if it isn't in the Bible, it isn't. We liked it there. The music was great, and the preaching was something we could understand. We made friends. Walt and Marcia were special. They came to visit. Walt and Chuck seemed to hit it off, being both Navy guys helped. They could talk about their Navy days.

When we had to refinance to pay the bills and had to do some repairs on the house before we could get a loan, Walt, also retired and not in A-1 health himself, helped Chuck. A couple other guys from Grace Church also helped with the repairs. By then, Chuck was feeling his health issues. Even though he tried to be macho, it showed. He would get very short of breath, then sit down and smoke another cigarette. He knew they were killing him. He tried many times to quit but couldn't.

I do believe that God sent us to that church. Chuck had been actively searching for God. Perhaps I didn't help by insisting on my way. Thankfully, I heard a quiet voice tell me to listen to Chuck.

Chuck knew he was not doing well. Still he tried to keep it from me. But how could I help but notice? He could barely walk anymore. We got a wheelchair from Four Points, and his kids came home from the Upper Peninsula and Maine. He knew he had to give up guardianship for Roger. When we went to court, he wanted to walk, but we took the wheelchair. Good thing too. If I remember correctly, Laurie drove us. Walking around the court was long. I remember Laurie pushing Chuck in the wheelchair, and we had to wait in the waiting area at court for quite a while. The home where Roger was living brought Roger. He limped badly but made it. If it hadn't been for Laurie and Linda, we must have been a pretty sad bunch.

The last picture we got of the family was at Roger's a few days later with Chuck and the kids. It still makes me cry. Laurie made me a big framed version of that picture. I wanted Roger to have something to help him remember his family, so I gave it to him. He better appreciate it because I wish now that I still had it. I can't remember if I drove that day or if Chuck drove, but I do remember he was in pretty bad shape. The girls went back home, but not long after that, he passed as I wrote about previously. The girls came back for the memorial.

The funeral was amazing. I didn't expect very many people, but they packed the church. My son-in-law Paul sang. Chuck's kids gave a testimony through their tears, and I was numb. The saddest thing, Chuck's cousin, his very good friend, got a call while there that his mother had passed. Aunt Frances had been like a second mother to Chuck but had spent her last days in a nursing home.

25

A couple weeks after he passed, my girls and I thought I should sell some of his stuff. He had many tools in the garage. We started to get together a garage sale. During that time, I had an idea for more tables out there. I was also purging in the house. I kept thinking, *There is no one here. I need to carry my phone just in case.* It seemed urgent that I have the cell phone with me. So I rigged a sock and a belt so I could carry it. I think that voice or thought knew I would be stupid.

One day, I decided to set up the tables I was thinking of. To do that, I had to move a very heavy plank. I heard voices in my head. *You can do this.* And another one said, *Don't try it.* After thinking those thoughts a few times, I decided to go ahead and move the planks. Well, I slipped and moved wrong. I popped my hip replacement out. No one was there. I was unable to move and in terrible pain. Thankfully, I had the phone, or I would have laid on that garage floor for who knows how long. I was able to call 911 and get help. I got an ambulance ride. The hospital emergency was amazing and popped my hip back in after they put me to sleep. Shortly, I woke up with no pain and able to walk on that hip. They sent me home. By then, they had called my girls. Then Susan took me home to my house. A week or so later, when we were pricing things for the sale, Susan was there. I reached down to write a price on something. It was low, so I stretched a bit extra. The hip popped out again. Sue caught me and lowered me to the floor. Another ambulance trip and the hip was back in place. We had the sale in early May. The girls did most of the work.

I was careful to use the walker and kept struggling to get things done. Then one day, I reached under a table to pick up a piece of fabric that had fallen. Oh no, pop again. I was able to stand on the good leg and lean forward, laying my upper body on the table. I couldn't reach the walker, and the pain was getting worse fast. Letting the bad leg sort of hang, I managed to slide myself along the table to the walker and somehow sit myself on the seat of the walker. I was then able to get my phone and call for help. The doors were locked. When they got there, they had to break in to the front door. The dispatcher had kept me on the phone and got permission for them to break down the door. Another ambulance ride. My girls must have been tired of running to the emergency by then, but those that could were there again. This time, a hip brace was ordered for me. I was afraid the hip would give out again, so I kept the brace on longer than the doctor wanted me to. He did say I could wear it forever if I wanted. So I planned to because I was so afraid.

Somewhere there, I lost track of time. Two months after I lost Chuck, Susan lost Paul. Most of that time was a blank in my mind.

What I do remember is, about a year later, Susan saying, "Mom, I have got this big house all to myself. You may as well come live in the lower level." The other girls kept encouraging me to do just that. I realized I could not keep up the house payments and was physically unable to even keep up the yard, much less any other maintenance. I finally consented to move.

I was able to pack and sort my own stuff. It took me a month. The next thing you know, it was the week before Thanksgiving, November 17. My family came and moved me to my daughter's lower level. They are one efficient bunch. They had my stuff loaded into a trailer in no time. And then at Sue's, unloaded in an unbelievable amount of time. The kids even helped me unpack while I was in a daze. They saw to it the bed was made and I had what I needed to cook. Of course, there were many things I didn't need right away, like my sewing, but I wanted to get things organized as soon as possible. So I worked at it. I am sure I did too much bending and lifting. I pretty much got it all done by Christmas. We had our traditional Christmas celebration on New Year's day in my space. By then, I was in much pain. I was blessed to have the best place any old lady could want. In it was plenty of room for a gathering of about thirty people. The windows overlooked a beautiful view of a good-sized pond and trees. People heard me say, "If I complained, I should be spanked." I think I know how

Job felt at the end, after losing everything then having it replaced and more.

I don't remember how long it was until I woke up one night in terrible pain. I think the brace had shifted and pulled on my back and popped out three vertebrae. I thought I just pulled muscles, so I waited a few days but finally couldn't take the pain and went to a chiropractor. She didn't do x-rays but just tried to adjust me from feel. I went a couple times more and decided she wasn't helping, so Sue took me to one who did x-rays. By then, I was in agonizing pain. In a couple days, we went for the x-ray results. He showed me and Sue where the compression fractures were and gave me some meds to strengthen my bones and help with the constipation that I was also suffering. He told me he didn't want to do anything right then but if I wanted, I could heal and come back in six weeks.

The bowel stuff helped but the back pain was bad and I could not lie in bed. I was sleeping in the recliner. The pain was so bad, I couldn't even hold a book. Then Sue drove me to Mercy Emergency, and they sent me to the orthopedic walk-in clinic. I am not sure about the order of things. They gave me a brace that was more painful for my back. I could not wear it. Finally, Dr. Hamati did surgery. He put cement inside the three vertebrae to hold them up, and I was nearly pain-free. This was about February 2019. I was not getting around good yet and still sleeping in the recliner. At a follow-up, they asked if I thought I could use therapy. I said yes. So I went to therapy which happened to be about one mile from where I live.

The therapist encouraged sleeping in bed, walking, and not using the walker. He put me through the paces, then told me there was no reason I couldn't drive, so I did a little. After ten weeks, I felt like I was getting my life back and was nearly pain-free. After discharge, I intended to keep up with what he showed me. But I gradually got lax, and pain started coming back. Now I am trying to do more all the time like he showed, but some days, the pain is a bit much. I sit a lot, then try to do things and many times too much. But I can read and sew and puzzle and cook. I can do my own housework, but somedays I have to force myself. I have learned through this that TV is a waste of time, and if one can't do things, life gets pretty boring. Where do I go from here? Remains to be seen, but I know that if I have to live with pain or am unable to take care of myself, I wouldn't want to keep going.

There is so much more I could write. If I did, this would never be finished. As I look over my life, I think that I lived in the best of times. Things are happening so fast that keeping up is near impossible. However, I continue to be spoiled because of all the technology and blessings.

I see God working every day. Looking back, God's hand has been on me from the beginning. Most of the time, I didn't appreciate it. Now I know that he is all that really matters, and his word holds the answers.

Afterword

Today is January 9, 2020. I looked out the window and what I thought I saw were geese walking on water; some were swimming nearby. Then I realized that what I saw were geese walking on clear thin ice.

Today is January 15, 2020. I am excited to work on a mystery quilt. It is a challenge. Yesterday, Diane, Doreen, and Jan came. We had a good time sewing and chatting. I don't go away much due to pain. If I sit long in chairs that don't fit, my back wants to cramp up. I still have some pain, but at home, I can move around more. Just working through a bout with sinus, ear, and balance problems. No fever.

I want to write my story but fear I won't finish or it will be dumb. I can self-publish it for family only but haven't looked into that. I do know that I need to edit and reedit it to make it worth reading. At this point, it's more of an outline. No feeling or description to make it interesting. I am torn between sewing and writing.

It's January 16, 2020. A strange thing happened. I went to gather up my trash to take out for tomorrow's pickup. It was all gone. I knew there was a cookie monster, but I've never heard of a trash monster.

January 20, 2020. I prayed to God that I couldn't get motivated to write. I asked him for inspiration. What I got was, "Just write. I will inspire you as you go."

April 1, 2020. In all my eighty-one years, I don't remember anything like this. Two weeks of no school and most everything shutdown. Groceries and pharmacies are still open. Everyone is requested to stay home, and people all over are sick. The coronavirus seems to be everywhere. I myself am weak and have a sore throat and headache for days. Along with that, the rash I have been battling for years is worse. Not much fun. Fighting the depression that wants to overtake me and just want to cry. Sue is dealing with what to do about the excavating. They are kind of in between. They have to determine if their business is essential or not. Some is, some is not. Don't feel like doing anything. Even writing is a chore. Don't like most TV, and reading is not what it usually is. Seems the whole country is shutdown.

Today is May 4, 2020. We still are under social distancing due to the coronavirus. I woke up feeling useless, in pain, and itching. Thankfully, Sue sat down and talked with me for a bit. At least I got motivated to move. Am doing a little laundry and working on my story. I think that I can't die till it's done, so I have to get busy on it. Something in my head said, *You will not die until you get your story done.* I still have half of it to write. The outline will not do.

Friday and Saturday, Joan, Sue, and Melissa came here to sew because the retreat they were planning to go to was canceled due to the virus. Yesterday, I watched church on

TV and the livestream of ours on the computer. Being tired of the restrictions, we had our usual every other Sunday dinner with Elizabeth and family, James and family, myself, and Ruth; all came to Sue's. We were a kind of family group that spent time together anyway. We had all been sick before the restrictions started. No one seemed sick any longer. It turned out to be a beautiful sunny day, so we got to enjoy the outside.

May 19, 2020. This morning, before I sat down to write, I filled the empty hummingbird feeder just outside the window. I barely got inside and turned around to look at it. There was a hummingbird inches from the window. As I looked at it, it started moving around like it was doing a dance. Was it trying to say thank you?

As I write this on May 28, 2020, the country is still under quarantine because of the coronavirus that has affected the world. Michigan more than most. People seem concerned that many small businesses will have to shut down due to loss of income. I am used to staying home, so it does not affect me much. But wearing masks at the store is not fun.

It's Monday, June first. Today we are hurting. A cop killed a black man, for whatever reason, we don't know. So now rioters are going into cities and making problems like looting and destruction. I don't know how that solves anything.

June 23, 2020. I have completed editing my story for the first time. I realize I have missed some things, so I will try to put them in where they belong, still editing what I wrote. It has been fun trying to write at least an hour every day. If the story is not good and boring, the kids will get it anyway. Hopefully, it will be printed by Christmas.

June 25, 2020. Christian Faith Publishing called yesterday. I don't think that she thought I would ever finish my story. What she doesn't know is I heard a voice that said, *You can't die until you finish your story.* Since I believe in God and heaven and am not excited to live with mild pain and limited ability, I got motivated.

June 26, 2020. It's as good as it gets. I am submitting this on Monday. Praise the Lord. Okay, I am nervous about sending this in. They are supposed to do self-publishing. But they also want to look at it before they accept it. So what does that mean? Where do I go from here? Along the way, I have written short stories and poems. I guess I could gather them together and see what I have.

It is August twenty-five 2020, It's my eighty-second birthday today. This is a true story of my life as best as I can remember. I realize I left many things out. Sorry. The world is crazy between coronavirus and politics. I am looking forward to going to my forever home. The Bible promises a better place with no pain. I know I have not led a perfect life but Jesus did. He is the only one that could pay my admission to heaven, He's my ticket and I can't wait. If I have to live another ten years the Holy Spirit will have to show me why I am still here.

About the Author

Mary Jean Rose is an eighty-one-year-old mother, grandmother, and great grandmother. This is her life story as she remembers it. She is now blessed to live with her daughter Susan in Grand Haven, Michigan, and have three other daughters nearby. She has been heard to say that she thinks she knows how Job felt near the end.

CPSIA information can be obtained
at www.ICGtesting.com
Printed in the USA
BVHW071801300121
599171BV00010B/175